This book may be kep
W9-ACQ-554

THE GOOD DUCHESS

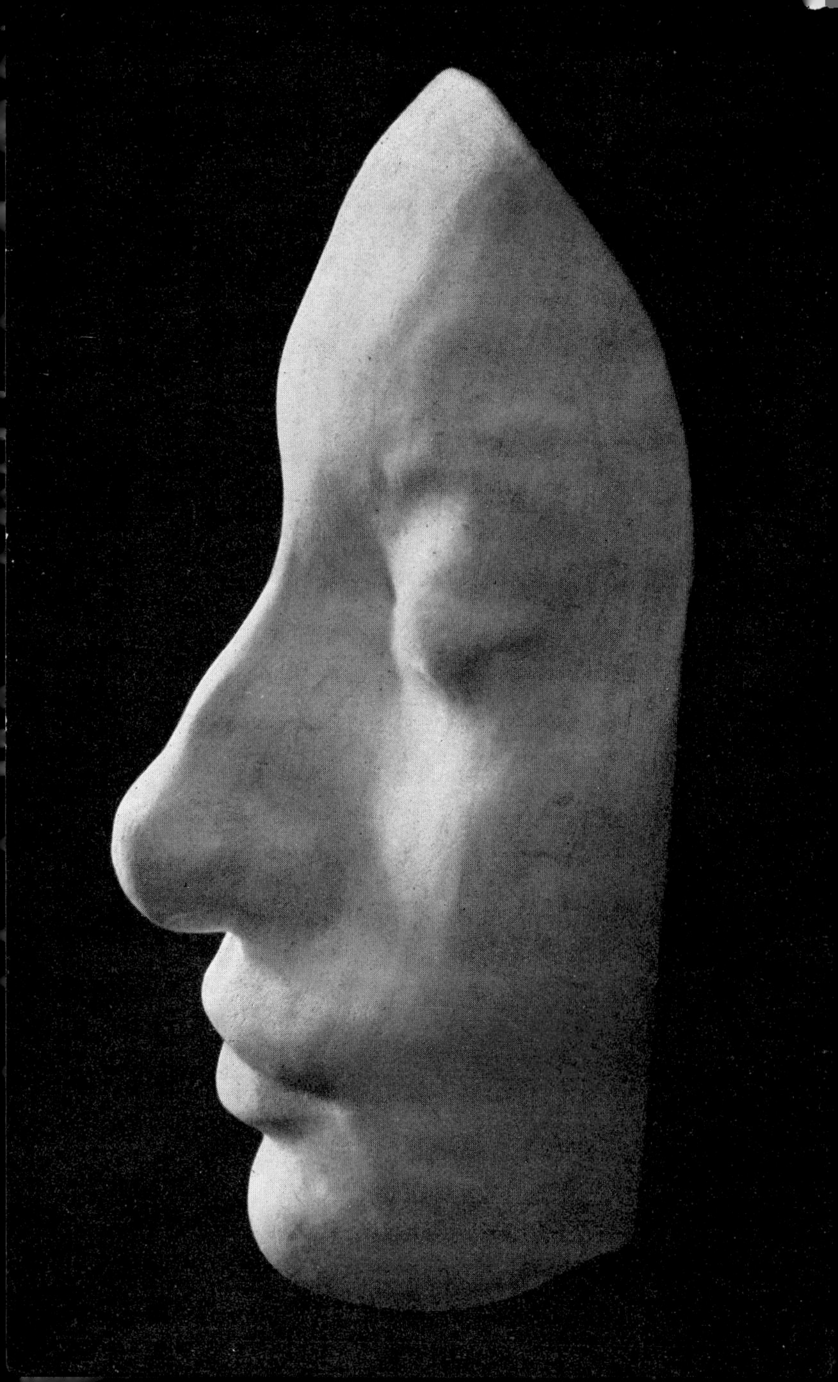

THE GOOD DUCHESS

Joan of France

(1464-1505)

by

ANN M. C. FORSTER

NEW YORK
P. J. KENEDY & SONS

P. J. KENEDY & SONS
12 BARCLAY STREET, NEW YORK 8

NIHIL OBSTAT: ERNESTVS MESSENGER, PH.D.
CENSOR DEPVTATVS

IMPRIMATVR: E. MORROGH BERNARD
VICARIVS GENERALIS

WESTMONASTERII: DIE XVIII FEBRUARII MCML

PRINTED IN GREAT BRITAIN

Dieu a les bras ouvers pour t'accoler,
Prest d'oublier ta vie pécheresse.
Requiers pardon. Bien te viendra aider
Notre Dame, la très puissante princesse
Qui est ton cry et que tiens pour maistresse;
Les saints aussi te viendront secourir
Desquels les corps font en toy demourance.
Ne vueilles plus en ton péché dormir,
Très chrestien, franc royaume de France!
Priez, prélatz et gens de saincte vie.
Religieux, ne dormez en paresse.

. . . .

Priez pour paix, le vray trésor de joye.

Lines written by Charles, Duke of Orleans,
during his captivity in the Tower of London,
1415–1440.

This Life of Joan of France was written in the expectation of her canonization at an early date. The author declares, however, that in designating her as saint, and in ascribing sanctity to her or to any other individual where this sanctity has not been confirmed by the Holy See, there is no intention of anticipating the judgment of the Church.

CONTENTS

FOREWORD

To attempt to write the life of Joan of France is to plunge at once into a sea of controversy. She has never lacked her biographers; and they have been of every conceivable shade of opinion. They range on the one hand from the extremists who hold that she was the legitimate wife and queen of Louis XII, repudiated by him for political motives by means of gross perjury and venality. At the other extreme are those who hold a brief for Louis XII and maintain that it was only after the removal of the incubus of his unhappy union that he was able to develop into the worthy king he afterwards became, the " Father of the People." Somewhere between these two extremes the truth lies. It has been my task to try to discover it.

Yet I have found that even against a shifting background the figure of Joan the saint remains constant. Whether she be wife unjustly repudiated or woman cruelly deceived, she remains patient, prudent, chaste—instinctively one applies to her those qualities of goodness which she made notable as the "Ten Virtues of Mary." It is worth mentioning that in the heat of the inquiry, when tongues were wagging freely with regard to her appearance and her physical disabilities, there was no hint of any disparagement of her dispositions or of her virtue.

I wish to acknowledge my indebtedness to the Abbé A. M. Destefanis, O.F.M., who in a recent work has reviewed all the factors, historical and judicial, involved in the case between Louis XII and Joan of France. It is his conclusion which, in the main, I have adopted.

I would like to thank also the Abbé J. F. Bonnefoy O.F.M., whose edition of the *Chronique de l'Annonciade* I have employed: Fr. Cassian, O.F.M.Cap., for help in bibliography: M. Antoine Redier for details regarding topography: and Mr. Gordon Smith for assistance in revision.

Above all I wish to express my gratitude to the Révérende Mère Ancelle of the Convent of the Annonciade, St. Margaret's Bay, and to the Very Rev. Canon Delpierre, chaplain to the convent, without whose help and encouragement this book could never have been written.

A.M.C.F.

CHAPTER I

OUR LADY'S GIFT TO FRANCE

WHEN Charles VII lay dying, in the summer of 1460, his son Louis, long estranged from him, was living in exile at the court of Burgundy. Louis had been an undutiful and rebellious son. As a young man, impatient of his father's periods of lethargy, he had intrigued with the great nobles and plotted to seize the government. In consequence he had been sent out of mischief's way, as it was hoped, and given the government of his own appanage, Dauphiny. There he had learned to govern. He had exacted the homage of his nobles, raised a regular army, organised commerce, remade roads in ruinous condition after a hundred years of war. He had made it his object to win the confidence of the middle classes, the merchants and men of money. He had been successful in his task. Dauphiny was well governed and prosperous; but Dauphiny was not France.

Following upon the discovery of some of his political intrigues, Louis had been obliged, in 1456, to fly from Dauphiny and seek refuge with the Duke of Burgundy in Brussels. Duke Philip, his kinsman, maintained a court unequalled in magnificence by any other court in Europe. He was one of the great vassals of the Crown of France, but the homage he paid to the King was of a very nominal nature. In his own dominions he exercised absolute sovereignty. The house of Burgundy, like many of the other great houses of France, was chafing under the bonds which held it in vassalage, and this jealous struggle for independence was at the bottom of much of the strife which Charles VII and his successors had to encounter during their efforts to unify France and establish a strong central government.

Louis had little to lose by the death of his father. There had long ceased to be any affection between them. As the news of the King's illness came through, he took horse and came as far as Avesnes, on the road to Rheims. There he waited with impatience for his father's end. On August the 3rd, the King's Requiem was sung in Avesnes. As soon as it was over, Louis set out hot foot for Rheims.

At seven o'clock on a summer evening Louis entered the city. He was splendidly attired for the occasion. His clothes were of red and white satin, his bonnet of cramoisy velvet. He rode upon a horse draped with cloth of gold, a canopy borne over his head. Accompanying him was the Duke of Burgundy. They paid a short visit to the cathedral on their way to the palace, and at midnight the King returned to the cathedral and kept vigil there until morning.

What were the thoughts that throbbed in that keen, dominating brain during those hours of darkness? Exultation foremost, that now at length the day was dawning when he, sanctified by the holy anointing, would lay hand to the task for which his fingers had itched so long, the remaking of France. His father had done much to restore order out of the chaos resulting from the Hundred Years' War. The English were gone: of the wide lands held by them only forty years earlier, nothing now remained to them except the city of Calais. The troops of foreign mercenaries, disbanded by all parties and left to wreak their will upon the countryside, had been collected and escorted out of France. Many churches and monasteries, laid low during the years of war, were rising again from their ruins. Towns and villages which had been almost entirely deserted, had been repopulated. Fields, overgrown with weeds and briers, had been cleared and replanted. France was beginning to breathe again the pure, sweet air of peace; but Louis, riding in from the rich lands of the Low Countries, had noted with sorrow the poverty of France.

Perhaps in this hour, as in no other hour of his life, there blazed up in the heart of Louis that fierce love which was to be his dominating passion—the love of France. It has been cast up against this man, this truly great king, that he had no heart, no religion: that he strove after his own ends, thrusting cruelly out of his way all who dared oppose him ; that he practised a form of worship which concerned itself with externals, with visits to shrines, veneration of images, gifts to churches. Much of this is true. All this he did, but he did more: he performed with every ounce of his weight, and every gift of his nature, the charge which God had entrusted to him, the care of France. France: in that hour of vigil in the cathedral he might have termed her his Lady France! The money wrung from his subjects he squandered, not in luxurious living, not upon himself at all, but on France, buying land, buying service, buying men. The policy which he deemed necessary for the good of France he pursued, regardless of his own ease or the distress of others. For France he was ready to sacrifice himself, his house, and all that belonged to it. Less than this he would not do for God. All of this he did for France.

At dawn the King made his confession and received Holy Communion. Then he returned to the palace to rest.

By nine o'clock the streets were packed with excited crowds. Outside the cathedral the great nobles were gathering, headed by the Duke of Burgundy, splendid in cloth of gold. The King was back in the cathedral now, waiting and praying. Suddenly a fanfare of trumpets was heard, and a procession was seen approaching: the Abbot of St. Rémy, bearing the sacred *ampulla*, the holy oil which for a thousand years had anointed the kings of France. As the great west door was thrown open, the King came down from his place and venerated the holy relic. The nobles, Burgundy, Bourbon, Dunois and the rest, flocked in, and the great ceremony began.

The solemn oaths were taken, the *Te Deum* sung. The King was anointed: forehead, eyes, mouth, shoulders, arms and body were dedicated in turn to the glory of God and the service of France. He was vested in the ceremonial robes, the shirt of rose-coloured silk, the doublet, the surcoat, the coat of azure. After this came the royal mantle, the golden spurs, the ring, the sword, and the sceptre. Last of all, the Duke of Burgundy lifted the crown aloft so that all might see, and set it upon the head of the King, crying out in a loud voice, "Vive le Roy! Montjoye Saint Denys!" and from the crowded cathedral came back the answering roar, "Vive le Roy!"

Louis XI was thirty-eight years old at the time of his crowning. He had been married, nine years previously, to Charlotte, daughter of the Duke of Savoy. She was his second wife. His first, married in extreme youth, was Margaret, daughter of James I of Scotland. It was a marriage of policy, and turned out unhappily. She died young. This time he had made the match himself, without reference to the King. It had not helped to heal the breach between them.

The little princess, only twelve years old at the time of the marriage, was one of the eighteen children of Louis of Savoy and Anne of Lusignan. The royal family of Savoy was noted for the piety and simplicity of its members. Duke Amadeus IX, the brother of Charlotte, and his daughter Louise of Savoy, are both venerated as Blessed: and Amadeus VIII, Charlotte's grandfather, was hardly less remarkable.

This prince, after the death of his wife, Mary of Burgundy, resolved to become a hermit. He waited until his son Louis was of age, and then he abdicated, and built himself a hermitage. It was a strange hermitage, a castle standing on the bank of a stream, and it was made with seven towers where he himself and his six companions, all like himself widowers, and all Tertiaries of St. Francis, lived together. They called the place Ripaille.

It was the time of the schismatical Council of Basle. The divines assembled there, being determined to exert their authority in the face of Pope Eugenius IV, decided to set up a Pope of their own. Their choice fell on the ex-Duke hermit Amadeus. He, in all good faith, was ordained, and reigned for nine years, under the name of Felix V. Then, realising the impropriety of his position, he retired and returned to his hermitage at Ripaille.

There a new rôle awaited him. Duke Louis and his wife Anne, both exemplary characters and Tertiaries of St. Francis, had, as we have noted, eighteen children. The Duke was frequently ailing, and much of the conduct of his affairs fell to his wife. She, poor lady, found that the care of a duchy in addition to eighteen children was rather more than she could manage. So she took seven of them, and sent them off to their grandfather.

Under his care and that of their governess they led a simple, happy-go-lucky life, running about in clogs, riding their horses, learning to look after themselves, and getting a thorough grounding in the practice of their religion. One of them was the little Charlotte who, on March the 9th, 1451, was married, at Chambéry, to the dauphin Louis. Five years later, being now seventeen years of age, she joined her husband at Namur, and with him was fêted and made much of in the gay land of Burgundy. In 1458 was born their first child, who did not live.

Louis longed for a son. Always devoted to the Blessed Virgin, he began to implore her assistance in this matter. He vowed to her that if she would obtain for him the gift of a son, he would give him the name of Joachim, in honour of our Lady's father, and his second child, who would be a daughter, he would call Anne, after her mother. On July the 27th, 1459, Joachim was born, and all the bells were set ringing in his honour. There was great rejoicing and feasting; but only four months later the little prince was laid to rest in the Church of Our Lady of Hal, on the outskirts of Brussels, a place of pilgrimage to this day. The following year the dauphine Charlotte gave birth to a daughter, whom Louis, faithful to his vow, named Anne. That same year he succeeded to the throne in the place of Charles VII, his father.

Here was Louis, a king without a son. The heir-presumptive was his brother Charles, Duke of Berry, a youth twenty years his junior, who had grown up to be his father's darling in the years while Louis had been away in Dauphiny and Burgundy. Next in succession was Charles Duke of Orléans, cousin to Louis' father. He was an old man now, notable as a poet. In extreme youth he had married the French princess Isabelle, child-widow of the murdered Richard II of England. He had been dragged out, more dead than alive, from underneath a heap of men, horses, and armour, hopelessly bogged in the drenched fields of Agincourt. After a captivity of twenty-five years in England he had returned to France, remarried and become the father of a young family. Two years after Louis came to the throne, the Duchess of Orléans, Marie of Clèves, presented her husband with a son.

Then followed fresh prayers and vows to our Lady

on the part of the King. Greater than ever grew his longing for a son an heir of his own body, one to whom he could teach that art of kingship which he himself had mastered with so much toil. Charles of Berry was no heir to his liking. Already history was repeating itself, and Charles was playing the game which Louis had played in his youth, deep in intrigues against the Crown, hungry for personal aggrandisement. In 1464 a formidable combination asserted itself. The Dukes of Berry, Burgundy, Brittany and others, incensed at Louis' methods of government, formed themselves into the "League of the Public Weal." That same year the Queen was expecting another child. This time it would be a son! Our Lady of Cléry, whose church he had rebuilt, Our Lady, who understood the needs of France, would hear his prayer, and send him a son.

Our Lady of Cléry heard his prayer, but she answered it in her own way; for when, on April the 23rd, 1464, Queen Charlotte gave birth to a child, it was not a son, but a daughter: Joan of France.

CHAPTER II

INFANCY

THE child was born at Nogent-le-Roi. This charming old town stands on a branch of the Eure, halfway between Maintenon and Dreux, in a country of green fields and shady trees. It has interesting historical associations. The very name recalls the fact that once, in August, 1350, five kings met together here: Philip VI of Valois and the kings of Navarre, Bohemia, Scotland and Aragon. It is a town of narrow winding streets, oak-beamed houses, centuries old, and leaning high-pitched roofs. The castle, dating originally from the 11th century, had been rebuilt by Pierre de Brézé, to whom it was granted by Charles VII, in return for services rendered during the English wars. He had pulled down the old castle and made himself a magnificent residence. For some time out of favour with the new king, whom he had opposed in the past, he was eventually reconciled and had his estates restored. Recently a match had been made for his eldest son, Jacques, with Charlotte of France, the King's half-sister, daughter of Charles VII and Agnes Sorel. This royal marriage had been celebrated at Chinon, and when Charlotte de Brézé's son was born, the King and Queen sent felicitations and presents. Now we find them staying at Nogent as visitors.

Why this was so at this time, we cannot know for

certain. Nogent is near Chartres, and it was a pious custom for the Queens of France to visit the shrine of our Lady of Chartres and pray for her blessing and protection in childbirth. It may have been on the way to or from Chartres that the King and Queen found it necessary to stop at Nogent.

There, at all events, the child was born; and there, presumably, she was baptised. There was no rejoicing or bell-ringing on this occasion. The King was deeply chagrined. He already had a daughter. By the law of France she could not succeed to the throne. What need of another, when his whole soul craved for a son? It seems as though he never forgave this child for her initial crime of coming unwanted into the world.

She was given the name of Jeanne, in English Joan. It was not an uncommon name. There must have been many little Jeannes in France during the years which followed the glorious exploits of Joan of Arc. Louis the King would just remember her, for he was six years old when she came to Chinon to speak to the King, his father, and start him upon the road to victory. Charles VII gave the name to two of the daughters he had by his Queen, and to one of those of Agnes Sorel. Louis XI in his youth had a natural daughter, also christened Jeanne; now he and Charlotte chose the name again for their younger daughter.

In spite of his disappointment at the new arrival, and the busy life he led, Louis did not hurry away from his wife's side. He stayed at Nogent three weeks, before going on to Paris. "On Tuesday the 15th May," the chronicler John of Troyes tells us, "the King arrived in his town of Paris, coming from Nogent-le-Roy, where the Queen was delivered of a fine child." Louis was engaged on important state affairs. He was on his way to the borders of Picardy, where he had appointed to meet the English and Burgundian envoys, to ratify a treaty of Peace, and to win back, at the cost of good French gold, the towns of the Somme.

During the month at Nogent, however, he had not been idle; far from it. He had lain in train a series of events which was to have a far-reaching effect upon the life of the little Joan. She might not be the heir he looked for, but still she was a Princess of France, and as such was of value as a matrimonial asset. Charles of Orléans, second in succession to the throne, had a young son: Louis had a baby daughter. What more suitable than a match between them?

No time was lost. The deed regulating the conditions of the betrothal was drawn up at the castle of Blois, the residence of the Duke of Orléans, and signed by the Duke himself, and by Jean de Rochechouart, representing the King. It was dated the 19th May. The bride-to-be was then just twenty-six days old.

A few months later, Charles of Orléans passed away, leaving his children under the guardianship of their mother, Marie of Clèves. The King was much engaged in putting down the League of the Public Weal, and had little time to devote to domestic affairs, even had he been so disposed. His children were left to their mother's care, living in the castle at Amboise.

Charlotte was now a woman of twenty-five, far removed from the gay young bride of Brussels days, and even more so from the little tomboy of Ripaille. Nevertheless, she had forgotten nothing of her early training. She taught her little ones to obey, to love God, to say their prayers. The impression which she made upon them in those days of infancy was never to be effaced. Moreover she passed on to them, even in nursery days, the sweet spirit of St. Francis which had come to her as the heritage of her race. To realise Christ, the God-made-Man, to know his nearness and the love he has for all his creatures, to have a tender affection for him and for his holy Mother: all this, in ways that they could understand, she imparted to them.

At Amboise, quite near to her, there was a monastery of Franciscans of the Colletine reform. The Father Guardian, Jean de la Fontaine, became her friend. She was generous in her donations to the monastery, as she was in all things. Years after her death, people recalled the charity which Queen Charlotte showed to the sick and needy.

Her household, though she maintained a royal state—there were more than forty domestics assigned to the service of the kitchen and table alone—exhibited none of the scandalous frivolity which was manifest in many of the great houses of the day. Her tastes were simple. Entertaining the numerous members of her family, making excursions in her litter, or riding the palfrey which the Bishop of Rheims gave her, seeing to her household or her dairy-farm, looking after her children, she had no lack of occupation. Moreover she was fond of reading. There was a collection of manuscripts in the library at Amboise, and these she loved to study and illuminate.

A sad day arrived for her, when Joan was about five years old. The King, for reasons which are not known to us, took a decision. The Queen and her elder daughter were to go to Dauphiny, Joan was to be placed in the care of a guardian. There is no reason to suppose that this decision implied any negligence or malice on Louis' part. It may have been in the child's own interests; but it meant a sad parting for Charlotte. Henceforth Joan was to see her mother only from time to time and never for long; but by the merciful dispensation of God, she was to find a second mother, no less true and tender than her own.

CHAPTER III

CHILDHOOD

FRANCOIS de Beaujeu, Baron de Linières, and his wife, Anne de Culant, were the guardians to whom the little princess was entrusted. He was descended from a family of high rank and, at one time, great possessions. In his veins ran the blood of Savoy, for Leonore of Savoy, cousin to St. Louis, was his ancestress, who, like others of her house, had a great devotion to the Poor Man of Assisi, and willed to be buried in the grey habit of his Order. But the domains of Beaujeu had been forfeited by an ancestor who was no credit to his lineage. The lands were confiscated and given to the Bourbons, and the Beaujeu family became greatly reduced. It was only the marriage of François de Beaujeu's father with the rich heiress of Linières which restored their prosperity and made François, in right of his mother, Baron and owner of the lands and castle of Linières, twenty-five miles from Bourges, in Berry.

Anne de Culant, Baroness de Linières, was also of noble birth, coming from the family of Chateauneuf-sur-Cher, which gave many notable men to France. She and her husband were an elderly couple and childless, and very ready to love and care for the little girl entrusted to them.

Of the castle of Linières which Joan knew, nothing except the church remains today; but from accounts which survive it is possible to reconstruct it.[1] There is nothing to suggest, as some of Joan's biographers have suggested, that this Gothic castle was gloomy and menacing. In the eyes of contemporaries it was a beautiful and sumptuous dwelling. Fifty years later, Catherine de Linières was to say of this same place: "Linières holds me in sway, it is my pleasure." Built in the days of St. Louis, it was surrounded by a moat, filled from the river Arnon, a tributary of the Cher. Passing over the drawbridge, one entered through a massive gateway into an outer court. Here were the guardrooms and stables, the workshops and the great watchtower. A second drawbridge and gateway gave entrance into the principal court. At one side of this stood the great donjon, with a winding staircase in the middle giving access to four storeys, and large rooms to right and left on each floor. The magnificent hall, with its tall windows, was easily capable, we are told, of seating five hundred persons. Its numerous other rooms were beautifully and comfortably arranged: its kitchens and offices proportionately spacious.

A trifle overpowering, perhaps, by puny modern standards, but a royal residence for the daughter of a King.

To Linières then came, about the year 1469, the little five-year-old princess. The elderly couple who received her gave her every care and loving attention. Whether she had many companions of her own age,

[1] See Antoine Redier—*Jeanne de France*

we have no means of knowing, but there must have been many children in the large establishment contained within the castle walls. One playmate she had, whose name we know. This was young Louis de Trémoille, afterwards a famous soldier of France, whose home was at Bomiers, not far away. He paid frequent visits, with his parents, to Linières, and it is in his biography, by Jean Bouchet, that we find a description of Joan at this period. She had a slight bodily ailment, he tells us, but a lovely face with beautiful eyes, greenish in colour and very deep and luminous. Her hair was fair and covered her shoulders.

She was a pious, obedient child, and very intelligent. In the long quiet days at Linières she learned to live as children do, in the company of her own thoughts, with this difference, that in her, thought tended naturally towards God. She talked to him, quite simply, of all her affairs and doings. He was ever present and very real to her.

The chapel which was attached to the castle still exists. It was desecrated and partly destroyed by the Huguenots during the Wars of Religion, but it has been carefully restored and now serves as the parish church of Linières. The sanctuary and transepts were undamaged and remain as they were in Joan's day. The transept on the left or Gospel side forms a little side chapel, separated from the sanctuary by a light colonnade of three arches. Two of the arches, those nearest the altar, are closed by a low balustrade of just such a height that a little girl could kneel and bow her head upon it. The third archway opens on to the sanctuary. This chapel was known as "the Ladies' Chapel." It had a door at the back, giving on to a corridor which connected it with the castle; and it was here, undoubtedly, that little Joan used to kneel, day by day, to hear Mass and tell her thoughts to God.

Another interesting detail. In this chapel, as one can see to-day, there was a large open fireplace for burning wood. It was a luxury in those days for a church to be warmed. Jacques Coeur, the famous merchant-prince, put several fireplaces into the chapel he built for himself, about this time, at Bourges. It is quite likely that François de Beaujeu followed his example and installed this one at Linières for the benefit of his royal charge.

Day after day she must have knelt against this balustrade, her back warmed by the blazing logs behind, her heart kindled by the burning love enthroned in the tabernacle before her. From her place she could see the altar, only a few feet away. She could watch the priest's profile, note every gesture of his hands and every movement of his lips. She knew, with all the faith and love of a child, what he was doing. When, at the sound of the bell, he lifted the Host high above his head, she recognised and worshipped Christ our Lord, and loved him with all her heart.

Over the altar hung the Crucifix. All her life Joan was to have a tender compassion for the Wounds of Christ, a devotion always associated in her mind with the burning love of Francis of Assisi. There was statue of our Lady, too. This particular statue was smashed when the church was desecrated. That which later replaced it is now three hundred years old: it represents the blessed Virgin seated, suckling her Child, a very human and touching Madonna.

Joan was six years old when one June morning in 1470, all the church bells rang joyously, and the people came out excited and jubilant, to fête a great event. Louis XI had a son! The long-looked-for heir had come, to his great delight and pride. The baby was born at Amboise and baptised Charles, the future Charles VIII. Joan was not present at the ceremony, which took place with the customary splendour.

Louis XI, in his sincere but somewhat restricted way, had a profound and lifelong devotion to our blessed Lady. As a young man of twenty, already an experienced soldier, he was taking part in the siege of Le Pollet, an outlying fort built by Earl Talbot, the English commander, for the purpose of reducing Dieppe. The fort, built on the top of a steep cliff, occupied a strong position overlooking the town, and Talbot's artillery was already working havoc there. On August the 11th the Dauphin Louis arrived before the walls of Dieppe. On August 12th he formally called upon the English to surrender. They answered that they were prepared to fight to the death. On August 14th the Dauphin laid his guns and issued a generous wine-ration to the troops. At 10 a.m. the battle began.

The position was strengthened with moats and manned by five hundred English with powerful cannon. For three hours under a blazing sun the French attacked, and were repulsed; renewed the assault and were again thrust back. At last they began to despair.

"Then," says Canon Médon, the historian of Cléry, who gives us this account, "the said Dauphin, finding himself in great consternation of mind and being destitute of all human aid, demanded of Jean, Comte de Dunois, 'Cousin, in which direction is Notre Dame de Cléry?' and being informed, cast himself down on his knees and vowed to our Lady of Cléry that if she would grant him victory he would rebuild the church (of Cléry), after the plans of his predecessor Philippe le Bel, and would enlarge and glorify it with great honour."

Over the water, as if in answer, came the chimes of the city's bells ringing in the First Vespers of the Feast of the Assumption. The Dauphin summoned his troops and made a final assault. This time he was victorious. He kept his vow, and rebuilt the church of Cléry, where his body rests.

It was in 1472, two years after the birth of his son, that Louis turned once more to our blessed Lady, to implore her to put an end to the troublesome strife in France.

"Henceforth," his order ran, "at the hour of midday, when the bell rings, let everyone bend knee to the ground and say *Ave Maria*, that she may give peace to the realm of France." So it came about that the midday bell would be rung at Linières, and all would repeat the Angelic Salutation.

The King made his daughter an allowance of 1,200 livres a year. With the varying values of money it is not easy to assess its corresponding value to-day. It is enough to say that it was a meagre allowance for a King's daughter, and this circumstance has been advanced as a proof of the indifference and hatred with which Louis regarded his younger daughter. It may not have meant anything of the sort. Louis, we know, was a parsimonious man. He may have considered that the child did not as yet require an establishment. Stories have been told, too, of how she went about in ragged frocks, and how the servants were not paid their wages. There may be something in all this, but, as we shall see later on, many of the stories of Joan's early life were exaggerated and distorted as the result of what came afterwards, so we must not attach too much importance to them.

One proof undoubtedly emerges of her father's interest in her welfare. He remembered that he was responsible for the care of her soul. It was he who, when she was six years old, recommended her to choose herself a confessor. A pious legend relates that, praying to our blessed Lady for light to make the proper choice, she became conscious of the answer: "My child, if you would love the Mother, go seek the Wounds of the Son." She took this to mean that she was to seek a confessor among the sons of the saint who bore the *Stigmata*, St. Francis of Assisi. In truth we know that devotion to St. Francis was in her very blood, and the confessor whom she chose was Father Jean de la Fontaine, her mother's friend at Amboise, whom she must have known from babyhood. He was her confessor for many years. Later on he was succeeded by another Franciscan, Father Gabriel-Maria, of whom we shall hear much during the latter years of her life.

Doubtful though this first revelation may be—she

nowhere refers to it herself—it was about this time that there occurred the incident she mentioned in later life to Father Gabriel-Maria. "One day," she says, "when I was hearing Mass—I was only seven years old at the time—it pleased God's mercy to reveal to me that before my death I should found an Order of Religion in honour of the Mother of God."

Another entry to the same effect is found in the Chronicle of the Annonciade, the story of the early days of the Order of the Blessed Virgin Mary. This chronicle, written by Sister Frances Guyard, was read and verified by Sister Marguerite Blandine, then a very old nun, who had been one of the first postulants of the Order and had been trained by Joan herself. The entry runs: "The said holy lady, being of the age of five [1] years, used often to pray to the Blessed Virgin Mary that she would be pleased to show her in what way she could do her service and pleasure: for it was her whole desire only to serve her and honour her and do her pleasure. And one particular day it seemed to her that the Virgin Mary spoke these words in her heart: 'Before thy death thou shalt found an Order of Religion in honour of me: and in doing so, thou shalt give me great pleasure and service.' "

It was a promise which the child never forgot. She kept it in her heart, mentioning it to no one. She did not see how it was to be accomplished. Neither, she remembered, did Mary understand "how this thing could be." With Mary, she answered: "Behold the handmaid of the Lord." With her, she was content to ponder in her heart,

[1] Actually seven years

awaiting the fulfilment of God's good pleasure.

About this time, in 1471, François de Beaujeu petitioned and obtained that his church might be raised to the rank of a collegiate church. The bull granting this favour, dated in the October of that year, was given by the Franciscan Pope Sixtus IV, the builder of the Sistine chapel in the Vatican. The bull gave permission for the church, hitherto the parish church, to rank as collegiate, with a dean and chapter. There were to be six canons, for whose endowment the baron undertook to be responsible. A difficulty arose in connection with the Benedictine monastery of Déols, upon which the church had hitherto been dependent. In 1473 the matter was arranged, and the King, at Plessis-les-Tours, confirmed the erection of a secular College, with all the customary honours, privileges and other advantages. François de Beaujeu, in accordance with the privilege granted him, nominated as the first dean Father Jean Raymond, the parish priest.

Linières received a further favour from the King in 1476. He granted to all the castle employees, as a special privilege, exemption from taxation.

The next event of which we have knowledge was that Joan had an illness. She took smallpox. We learn this from a letter, fortunately preserved, written by Queen Charlotte to one of the King's ministers.

"On behalf of the Queen.

"Monsieur du Boscaige,

"Madame de Linières has written to say that my daughter Joan has been ill of smallpox and has now recovered. She writes, too, that Monsieur de

Linières is extremely ill of fever, and she is anxious that I should send and take my daughter away in case any harm should come to her : as you can see by the letters which I am sending you by bearer ; by the same bearer I am writing to the King regarding this matter, that he may decide as he thinks best; for I dare not send and fetch my daughter without first referring the matter to him. I beg that you will convey my letters to my Lord the King and show him, if need be, the letter of Madame de Linières. And despatch the bearer as soon as you possibly can, so as to accomplish my lord's good pleasure, and let me know. Adieu. Written Amboise, the 17th day of July. Charlotte."

The answer to this letter has not been preserved, so we do not know what action was taken. Joan got back her strength, she was not marked by the small-pox, and as the baron also recovered, she continued to live at Linières, with occasional periods of residence at the baron's town house in Bourges.

What were her occupations at this time? She received, of course, the education suitable to a child of her period and rank. She learned to read and write. Before the days of printed books, this was an accomplishment confined to a minority of the people, the clerical and noble classes. She was well versed in the psalms; one of her first cares, on founding her Order, was to see that the postulants were similarly grounded. She learned to sew, to draw, to play the lute. (We shall see that lute again. Later on in life it broke, and out of a piece of it she contrived a novel implement of penance. Studded with points, she wore it pressed against her flesh.) Some specimens of her work have been preserved: little religious motifs painted in water-colour, representing the Crown of Thorns, the Cross, the Heart encircled with foliage and flowers, the kind of designs which were made for the purpose of illuminating manuscripts. We remember that this was a favourite occupation of her mother. There is, too, a little piece of cloth, established as her work, showing the monograms of our Lord and our Lady woven into the material. For the rest, we may picture her living in quiet, letting the sweet peace of the country sink deep into her soul: taking her walks abroad, hand in hand with the old man who loved her, among the green fields and by the shady lakeside. Berry was a pastoral country. As a chronicler tells us: "It serves right well for the pasturage and nurture of beasts, and particularly of sheep, which, since the temperature and sweetness of the air raise there a herbage which is very tasty and delicate, bear fleeces finer and softer than in any other part of the realm."[1] The people of Berry were sons of the soil; slow, quiet and wise. It was they, not the pleasure-loving nobles, who stood to gain by the policy of Louis XI. That great king had the wisdom and the charity to realise that when the leaders go to war it is the humble who suffer most. In dealing with conspirators and enemies it was always his way to strike hard at the heads of the movement, and let the rest go free. "He had much pity for the poor folk whose counsels might not prevail against the mighty," so the chronicler tells us, "for naught had the poor done of their own

[1] Nicholas de Nicholay, 1567, quoted by Redier.

accord." There would be old men who could remember the days when neither man nor beast was safe, except in the vicinity of a fortified place. They would recall the terrible doings of the soldiery, the burning of homesteads, the slaughter of cattle. They would have tales to tell of how Pierre's son was murdered, and Jean's carried away and pressed for the army: and how André, coming back from the wars, had everything to build up from the ruins. Many a time, meeting the little princess on her walks, they must have stepped aside with lifted bonnets, and praised God for the father of this little one, that was bringing peace to France. And as the *Ave Maria* rang out at midday, she too would pray for peace, not yet realising that one of the strongest cards which the King held in his hand, most potent factor for the union of France, was the marrying of his daughters.

CHAPTER IV

MARRIAGE

MEANWHILE at Blois, the young Louis, Joan's husband-to-be, was growing up in a very different environment.

His late father Charles of Orléans, after his return from captivity, lived there in princely style. Some years before his marriage he adopted his young kinsman Peter de Beaujeu, brother of the Duke of Bourbon, and brought him up as his own son. When, late in life, he had a family of his own, he affianced his first daughter to this prince.

Duke Charles died in 1465, leaving a young widow, Marie of Clèves, and three little children, Marie, aged seven, Louis aged two, and an infant daughter, Anne. Peter de Beaujeu, as his adopted son and the betrothed of his daughter, had the conduct of the funeral obsequies. These were very magnificent, and give some idea of the state and importance of the House of Orléans at this time.

"The Duke's remains were followed," the historian[1] tells us, "by four pages. Then came the innumerable members of his household, to wit, forty-three gentlemen, five priests, of whom two were almoners,

[1] Pierre Champion, *Charles d'Orléans*

thirteen choristers and the organist, the huntsman and fifty-two footmen, a surgeon, two apothecaries, two barbers, two painters, the smith, two tapestry-workers, two tailors, the lute-player, the bear-keeper, two kennel-men and eight grooms; then the kitchen folk, two cooks, an undercook, four cup-bearers, a pantler and four scullions. Last came the fool."

It was under these luxurious conditions that Louis of Orléans was brought up. His mother, Marie of Clèves, was a worldly woman, and, according to current gossip, speedily consoled herself for the loss of her husband with her familiar, Rabaudanges. Her youngest daughter Anne at an early age was appointed Abbess of Fontevrault, a lucrative and influential position. It seemed as though all three children were handsomely settled in life.

About 1473, King Louis found it necessary to take stock of his affairs and make certain decisions for the future security of the kingdom. Several recent events had contributed to this. In the first place, his brother Charles, who had given him much anxiety but who, mainly through the good offices of the Queen, had been formally reconciled to him in 1469, was now dead. Shortly after his death, in 1472, Queen Charlotte gave birth to a second son, Francis. The King was overjoyed at the happy event; but a year later, to his great sorrow, the infant prince died suddenly. He was buried in the church of the Friars Minor at Amboise. Meanwhile the Dauphin Charles was growing up, a feeble, delicate child. His life, and his only, stood between Louis of Orléans and the throne.

All this time, Louis XI was continuing his policy of working for the union of the different provinces of France under the Crown. To understand his difficulties we have to look back several generations, to King John II who, a hundred years earlier, divided up the kingdom between a large number of sons, maintaining only a nominal control. From him were descended the houses of Orléans, Anjou, and Burgundy, whose jealous rivalry had torn France in pieces, and kept her perpetually in a state of civil war. It was the constant aim of Louis XI to prevent a combination of any of these houses which might prove strong enough to menace the security of the Crown. The Bourbons, another powerful family, ought to have been sufficiently bound to him by the marriage of the Duke of Bourbon with Joan of France, the King's sister; but in the recent League of the Public Weal Bourbon had broken away and joined the other princes in conspiracy. Now it appeared that Bourbon's younger brother, Peter de Beaujeu, was about to contract a marriage with a branch of the royal house, that of Orléans. Louis decided that the two would be better apart.

The position of the young Duke of Orléans, too, gave him cause for anxiety. He stood, as things were, second in succession to the throne. Louis foresaw a dangerous rival for his own son, should that son succeed as a minor. He determined to curtail the power of the duke as far as possible. Orléans was already betrothed to Joan, his younger daughter, now a child of nine, retiring in character, delicate in health, and so misshapen that it did not seem likely that she could ever be the mother of healthy children. If Louis desired the extinction of the house of Orléans, here was an instrument ready to his hand!

It was a scheme worthy of his contemporary Machiavelli, almost incredible in its subtle brutality; but we have evidence of Louis' intentions in a letter written to his minister Dammartin, the authenticity of which is considered to be beyond dispute. The letter was as follows:

"To our beloved cousin Count de Dammartin,
Grand Master of France.

"My Lord Grand Master, I have seen your letters, and as far as your affairs are concerned, I shall not forget them, and do not you forget mine. I am sending your despatches by Pierre Cléret. My Lord Grand Master, I have decided to go on with the marriage of my little daughter Joan with the little Duke of Orléans, because I fancy that the children they will have together will not cost them much to rear. I advise you that I mean to accomplish this marriage, elsewise those who go contrary to me will have no assurance of life in my Realm, wherefore I am minded to carry out the whole according to my intention. Adieu, my Lord Grand Master. Written at Selommes, the twenty-seventh day of September.

"Loys (Tillart)."

Louis laid his plans accordingly. He broke off the match between Peter de Beaujeu and Marie of Orléans, and affianced that prince to his own daughter Anne. The young Duke of Orléans he held to his engagement with Joan; and now, in 1473, he prepared to make these marriages as binding as they could possibly be made, short of the actual religious ceremony.

The Duchess Marie of Clèves was greatly distressed at the trend of events. Rumour had reached her that Joan was neither as brilliant nor as good-looking as her sister. She had long entertained the hope that the King would change his mind and give her son the elder instead of the younger daughter, and in the course of the preliminary negotiations Louis seems to have taken a malicious pleasure in leaving her in her error. The shock, when she discovered the truth, was the greater. She resisted to the utmost of her power; but the King sent one emissary after another, uttering more and more violent threats of action against herself, her son and the members of her household should she refuse to accept the engagement on behalf of the duke.

It seems that, at this time, Louis had not seen his daughter for some years. He sent for de Linières, and questioned him with regard to her condition. De Linières assured him that the rumours concerning Joan were exaggerated. She was not nearly so deformed as people made out. The King, easily reassured, and in any case caring little, pressed on with his project.

It is not easy to determine the exact nature and extent of the physical disability under which Joan of France suffered at this time. Many historians have depicted her as ugly in features and badly deformed in body. They derive their facts from the statements made during the Suit for Nullity brought against her by her husband, then King Louis XII, twenty-five years later. At that time the scales of justice were tipped in favour of the King. The witnesses, who testified on his behalf with regard to her condition at the time of the marriage, had every encouragement to exaggerate, and probably did so. For instance, Louise Jarry, a nun, who had known Joan as a child and been a member of her household, speaking on behalf of the King, gave the following evidence:

" The Defendant," she said, "was deformed before her marriage, and she leaned to one side, and I have never seen anyone more deformed. Only to look at her, you would know she was lame."

However, apart from highly coloured evidence of this sort, there are other sources of information which give some idea of Joan's actual condition.

In the first place, we know that she was healthy at birth. "The Queen," the chronicler tells us, "was delivered of a fine child."

Next we have the description of her, already quoted, by Madame de Trémoille. "She was a little imperfect in body, but she had a lovely face." This is confirmed by the evidence given by La Palu, Joan's equerry: "She was crippled, but she had a fair enough face," he said.

We have the evidence of her death-mask. It is a thing which one cannot contemplate without emotion. An oval face, a big, irregular nose, a wide generous mouth, the lips firmly and sweetly set : there is not a single feature which is beautiful in itself, yet the whole bears the stamp of a beauty unmistakable. There is serenity here, strength, sweetness, radiance even. It is the face of a young woman, tired and worn out before her time, resigning herself, with all the abandon of a child, into the hands of her Eternal Father. That homely face, irradiated in life by the lovely luminous eyes, expressing all the traits of a beautiful character, must have been a thing to be remembered by men and women of discernment.

Next, we have her own evidence, given at the Nullity Process quite simply and humbly. "She knew," she said, "that she was not as fair or as well formed as most women."

In the Chronicle of the Annonciade she is twice described. The first description comes in the chapter relating the circumstances of the annulment. She is said to have been "of small stature and deformed in the shoulders."

The other description is very suggestive. It occurs in the passage which relates how she performed the ceremony of the Washing of the feet on Maundy Thursday. We must remember that this passage was read and approved by Sister Marguerite Blandine, who was an eye-witness of the ceremony in question. Here it is :

"When the hour came, the thirteen poor people were arranged and seated upon high benches, in such a way that Madame, who was very small in body, could stand up to wash their feet."

Why was this peculiar arrangement made ? Why did Madame have to stand up ? It is usual to kneel at the Maundy. It was not that she could not kneel, for only a few sentences further on she is described as kneeling with great devotion. It was not because she was short. It suggests rather that she could not *bend down*. In other words she had some stiffness of her spine.

There is also in the Chronicle, in a third passage, an allusion to her appearance. Her confessor related that in order to practise humility, she would compel him to call her all kinds of humiliating names: "*Humped*" was one of the epithets in question; and there would have been no sting in such an appellation unless it had been true.

What do we deduce from all this? That she was a healthy baby at birth, but developed in early childhood some disease which resulted in a spinal deformity and interfered with normal growth. As she grew older, of course, the shortening and deformity would become more marked.

Further than this we need not go. We need not accept, without question, all the exaggerated statements which were made during the Process, with the object of showing that she was unfitted for marriage. The King could command what witnesses he pleased, and the Queen did not hesitate to say so.

"The illustrious Lady Defendant declared," so runs the account of the proceedings, "that each and all of the said witnesses, before and at the time of their deposition were, and are, subject to the orders of the said Lord Claimant, that they are members of his household and, for the most part, his boon and sworn companions who, seeing that they are malicious and uncertain in their depositions, contradict one another, and make statements which are neither true nor probable, do nullify or at least impair the force of a part of their arguments, and render the rest wholly unreliable."

According to Claude de Rabaudanges, one of the witnesses in question, the threats of Louis XI grew more and more detailed. The duke was to be removed from his mother's control and sent into a monastery: she herself would be deprived of her dowry and banished the kingdom: her advisors would lose their heads. She was prevailed upon to temporise. After all, her friends pointed out, the duke and his future bride were still very young. Anything might happen before the actual marriage took place. In the end she signified herself willing to comply with the King's wishes. She even attempted, all too late, to reconcile her son to the match.

Louis of Orléans, now eleven years old, was a petulant, handsome boy, fast becoming a good athlete and an accomplished horseman. He was fond of pleasure and good living. His mother indulged him, and his little court at Blois flattered and pampered him. He was in many respects unfitted to be the husband of a girl as simple and pious as Joan. He resented the marriage from the very first, and as time went on his attitude grew more and more disdainful.

At Jargeau, on the 28th of October, 1473, Louis received Marie of Clèves. She came from her residence at Chateauneuf-sur-Loire close by, accompanied by John Vigneron, her treasurer, and others of her household, to discuss the settlements. The King received her in high good humour, and told her that the usual dowry of a Daughter of France was 100,000 livres, but that he proposed to assign to Joan a dowry of three times that amount. Vigneron in his testimony before the Tribunal did not hesitate to allege that the King added: " because Madame Joan is not as fair as the Duke and Madame his Mother could wish;" but the truth is that only five days later Louis assigned the same dowry to his other daughter.

The marriage contract was drawn up by two notaries. One copy was taken to Chateauneuf and read aloud to Marie of Clèves and her son. The conditions were accepted and the deed signed, everyone remarking upon the prudence and composure of the young duke. The contract stipulated that the religious marriage should be celebrated at such time as either party should require it of the other. It could not in any case take place for several years, for both were too young, the canonical age for marriage being fourteen years for a boy and twelve for a girl.

The next days were given over to feasting and rejoicing, so much so that, by special arrangement, the feasts of All Saints and All Souls were deferred, so as not to interfere with the festivities. On November the 3rd the same process was repeated and Anne, the King's elder daughter, was contracted to Peter de Beaujeu. For five days more the feasting continued.

It was only after the conclusion of this, the civil contract, that Marie of Clèves made the acquaintance of her future daughter-in-law. She came to Linières to visit her, and expressed her displeasure freely. According to the deposition of de Gié, the duchess was so overcome that she had to "have her laces cut." "Must my son marry this deformed girl?" she cried.

About the same time the King also decided to see

his daughter. "After the marriage contract was made," de Rabaudanges deposed, "King Louis wished to see his daughter, and the Sire de Linières brought her to Plessis where King Louis was . . . and on a certain morning the Sire de Linières brought her in, supporting her upon his arm, and the King saw her through the window: and thereupon he made the sign of the Cross, declaring that he had not thought her to be like this."

Three years later, in September 1476, the religious marriage took place, again a double wedding of the two sisters, at Montrichard.

The castle of Montrichard, of which only a ruin remains to-day, was a rocky fortress standing high above the river Cher. In the eleventh century it was the stronghold of Fulk Nerra (Fulk the Black), Count of Anjou, ancestor of Henry II and the Angevin kings of England. For Joan and her mother it would have many associations. During the Hundred Years' War, being on the direct route between Berry and Touraine, it was frequently visited by Charles VII. After peace was restored he paid several visits here, one of the most notable being in 1452, when he came on pilgrimage to the church of Our Lady of Nanteuil, which lay at the foot of the crag on which the castle stood. The following year, 1453, Montrichard was honoured with a visit by the Queen, Marie of Anjou, accompanied by a splendid suite of ladies and attendants. There had been a still more recent royal visit in 1461, shortly after the accession of Louis XI, when he and Charlotte came to take over this ancient fortress from its previous owners, the family of Amboise, exchanging for it other territories.

At Montrichard then, a spot convenient for all parties, the wedding-guests assembled, travelling from Chinon, Tours, Amboise, Blois, Orléans, Jargeau and Linières. Queen Charlotte came from Amboise, bringing the princess Anne, and great must have been her joy at having both her daughters in her arms. Joan of Bourbon came, sister of the King and sister-in-law of Peter de Beaujeu. He brought his sister Margaret and her husband Philip of Savoy, Charlotte's brother. The King was not present. He was engaged in offering thanksgiving for the victory gained by the Swiss over Philip the Bold of Burgundy. Madame de Linières of course was there, to see her darling married.

The Duke of Orléans was less well attended. His mother was not able to be present. She had selected this day, September the 8th, for the wedding of her daughter Marie, who was consoled for the loss of Peter de Beaujeu by a marriage with John de Foix. The duchess was represented by members of her household, by Vatan, the duke's governor, by his daughter Elizabeth, recently married to Fricon, the duchess's steward, and by Dunois.

The feast of the Nativity of Our Lady, 1476, was the day chosen for Joan's wedding. The dispensation granted by Pope Sixtus IV had been forwarded by the papal legate at Avignon, Cardinal Jules de Rovere, to the officiating bishop, Francis de Brilhac, Bishop of Orléans. The dispensation was necessary on two counts: the blood relationship between the contracting parties (Louis of Orléans was second cousin to Joan's father), and spiritual relationship (he was the King's godson). The bishop separated Louis and Joan, kept them apart for two hours to think over the marriage, and then questioned each of them in turn as to their readiness to enter into it.

Francis de Brilhac, who gave evidence at the Process, declared then that the Duke of Orléans when interrogated as to his willingness to marry, answered, "Alas! my Lord of Orléans, what can I do? I can not say No; it would be as much as my life was worth. You know with whom I have to reckon."

If Louis really spoke these words—and we cannot easily charge the bishop with perjury—then how could that prelate have found it in his conscience to go on with the marriage? Terrible indeed must have been the fear inspired by Louis XI!

So the wedding went forward. The little bride, wearing a robe of stiff black satin with an overdress and train of cloth of gold, which with her long fair hair and brilliant eyes must have looked striking enough, stood up beside her tall, sulky bridegroom. The solemn vows were taken, the bishop blessed them and declared them joined in holy matrimony. Then he turned abruptly and left them. He did not even stay for the nuptial Mass. He went, as he airily told the tribunal, to dinner at the Three Kings inn.

The next day the other couple were married, the celebrating bishop in their case being Charles de Bourbon, Bishop of Lyons, brother of the bridegroom. An unfortunate thing happened. They too needed a dispensation, and it did not arrive until after the wedding was over. Some scandal was caused, and the

Bishop was obliged to remarry them some time later. Their marriage had a sad beginning, but it turned out happily and well.

Joan's marriage also had a sad beginning. It was to have a weary continuation, and a bitter, humiliating end.

CHAPTER V

DUCHESS OF ORLEANS

SOON after the wedding, the Duke of Orléans and his wife paid a visit to Blois. This castle was his chief residence, for Orléans, the principal town of the duchy, had been badly damaged during the war and had not yet recovered.

It was a gay cavalcade. The little duchess was splendidly dressed for the occasion, young and radiant. The people of Blois gave them a great reception. If Louis, as was afterwards maintained, spent his wedding-day in tears, he managed on this occasion to conceal his feelings pretty successfully. At the Process he was interrogated on this point. Here are his answers:

"The Defendant deposes that after the said solemnisation and consummation of the marriage, the said Lord Claimant, then Duke of Orléans, caused the said Lady Defendant to enter into the town of Blois."

"He does not agree."

"She deposes that he caused her to enter as his wife and Duchess of Orléans."

"He does not agree."

"She deposes that it was with all the honours customary on such occasions."

"He does not agree."

Here, on the other hand, is Joan's statement:

"She deposes that, a little after the solemnisation and consummation, the said Claimant, then Duke of Orléans, caused her to enter into the town of Blois as his wife and Duchess of Orléans, and caused her to be received as a natural sovereign, that is to say the lawful wife of the said Serene Claimant, and that this entry was made with pomp and with great manifestations of joy; and that on this occasion he behaved freely and openly after the fashion customary at such ceremonies. And by his enjoyment of the marriage celebrations and his approval tacitly expressed, not so much by words as by bows and gestures, he showed that his presence there was voluntary and not involuntary, and that he was not labouring under any kind of fear or constraint."

Even after twenty-five years Joan could still hear the shouts of acclamation that greeted her on that occasion, and see the handsome lad caracoling at her side, laughing, waving his hat, greeting the roaring crowds. She remembered it and told of it, and her words are to be believed. For listen to another deposition of hers:

"The Defendant deposes that one who knowingly commits a mortal sin will suffer eternal damnation."

"She deposes that one who knowingly perjures himself, incurs the anger of God and merits eternal damnation."

She did not stay long at Blois. Very soon she was back at Linières, and there she was to remain for another seven years. There was nothing extraordinary about this. Joan was much too young to have an establishment of her own. She might indeed have made her home with her mother-in-law, as was customary with young brides, but Marie of Clèves was unwilling to receive her. The child looked so delicate, she said, that she would not care to be responsible for the charge of her. In any case her Court was not a suitable environment for one of Joan's character and tastes. Louis XI, who with all his shortcomings as a parent, at least retained some consciousness of his responsibility for her spiritual welfare, may well have considered that residence at the Court of Blois would profit neither her health, her happiness nor her morals. He may even have been influenced by a haunting memory of his own unhappy first marriage, and of the little Scottish bride who died broken-hearted amid the malicious gossip and crackle of a royal court. Joan would be far better at Linières.

She came back and resumed her old life, her quiet occupations, her hours of prayer; but now there was a difference. Now there was someone to pray for, someone who belonged to her in a very special way, for whose welfare she was, in a sense, responsible. Daily she prayed for grace to do her duty by him, to make him a good wife, to see him happy.

According to the deposition of de Gié, the King, being at Bourges, sent for his daughter. This was probably a few months after the marriage, in February 1477, when Louis XI paid a visit to the city, in connection with a dispute over the relics of St. Ursin. Again he expressed himself shocked at Joan's appearance, and declared that de Linières was " a fool and a sot" in deceiving him as to the extent of her deformity.

There is something a little suspicious here. This story, related by de Gié at the Nullity Process, bears a strong resemblance to the one already given, deposed by de Rabaudanges and referring to a similar event, but in another setting. It tends to throw doubt upon the veracity of one or other of them. If Louis was in truth horrified by the appearance of his daughter on the first occasion, when he saw her in de Linières' company, how could he have been so shocked the second time, and blamed de Linières for deceiving him ? On the other hand, both incidents may be true, and the lack of veracity may be found in the hypocrisy of Louis himself, attempting, now that the marriage was a *fait accompli*, to fix the blame for it on someone else.

He was insistent in compelling the young duke to visit his wife at frequent intervals. If he failed to do so, the King's messenger would arrive with a peremptory demand. Details given by many witnesses at the Tribunal paint for us a picture of the unhappy union of this unfortunate pair. Three or four times a year the quiet life at Linières would be interrupted. The duke would arrive, sometimes with his mother, sometimes with a train of companions, male and female. At these times all the rooms would be lighted up and the great banqueting-hall filled with a laughing, chattering crowd. There would be song and dancing, feasting and merry-making; but in the midst of all the throng the little duchess would sit silent and neglected. Her husband had scarcely a word for her. He was not even civil, turning his back upon her at table, the moment grace was over, and devoting himself to his other companions. If he gave her a minimum of attention, it was because the King's spies were everywhere, even, it was alleged, in the married quarters of the young couple.

Then one morning the horses would clatter away, the gold and silver plate would be packed back into its chest, the rooms would be silent and still; and the young duchess would go back to the church to make up her arrears of prayer, and to beg God's blessing on her gay young husband, that one day he might overcome his repugnance, and accept the marriage in the same spirit of resignation as she herself had accepted it.

As for Orléans, life could not give him enough. There must be balls, masques, theatrical performances not of the most edifying kind. There must be tourneys, shows of horsemanship, followed by banquets and revellings far into the night: flattery, dalliance with fair women, giving to others the place that should be hers. "I am *not* married!" he declared indignantly to one who ventured to reproach him.

So the years went by, and Joan must have wondered whether life was always to be like this.

She was fifteen years old when startling news came to Linières: the duke was in Bourges, lying sick of the small-pox. To the young duchess her duty as a wife appeared paramount. It took her straight to his bedside.

She arrived in Bourges, and found her husband's

mother and sisters already in possession. Neither they nor he gave her any welcome. It was a difficult position for a young and diffident girl, but Joan's gentle nature revealed unexpected reserves of strength. She remained in Bourges until her husband had recovered; then she returned to Linières.

When she was seventeen she had the grief of losing her dear foster-mother, Madame de Linières. After his period of mourning was over, the Baron took another wife, Frances de Maillé. No doubt she was all that was kind, but she could never replace the friend that was lost. Then, one day two years later, came news that sent Joan back to her knees: Louis XI was dead.

He died with the greatest reluctance. When he knew that he had not long to live, he sent for this relic and that, made promises and vows, called on every hand for prayer that his life might be prolonged. Finally, hearing of a holy old hermit in Calabria whose prayers were very efficacious with God, he caused him to be brought to his bedside. St. Francis of Paola was the saint who came to Plessis-les-Tours, and helped him, not to prolong his life but to prepare for death. As the end approached, he appointed Anne, his elder daughter, to be Regent of the kingdom, and recommended to her care and that of her husband his thirteen-year-old son, King Charles VIII. He summoned the Duke of Orléans, and made him take an oath upon the Gospels that he would be loyal to the new King and to the Regent Anne. Having put his affairs in order to the best of his ability, he received the Last Sacraments and made a good end, commending himself, with his last breath, to our blessed Lady. "My good Mistress," he whispered, "help me!"

Joan went to Amboise. Here her mother was living. The poor Queen was to follow her husband to the grave only a few months later. Here was Joan's young brother, Charles VIII, for whom she had a great affection, which he came to return with all his heart, and her sister, the Regent Anne, who received her with great kindness. Here too was their cousin Louise of Savoy, the dearly loved wife of Hugh of Châlons. She is now venerated as Blessed. At Amboise Joan found another, very young, princess, who had only recently left her home to come and be educated at the court of France as the future wife of its King, Margaret, daughter of the Emperor Maximilian. To this little princess Joan devoted herself. A strong attachment grew up between the two, an attachment which was never to weaken, and which was to have profound repercussions upon the future of the Order which Joan was destined to found.

There was another living at Amboise to whom her coming was less welcome, the Duke of Orléans, her husband. Even before the late King's death he had been deep in intrigue, seeking to carve out a domain for himself. The greater part of France was now reunited to the Crown. Picardy had been regained, Anjou ceded by King René in return for help granted to his daughter, the English Queen. Burgundy was annexed on the death of Charles the Bold, despite the protests of that prince's daughter, Marie. Only the dukedom of Brittany maintained its independence.

Louis of Orléans cast longing eyes upon this territory. The Duke of Brittany was an old man, and his successor would be a young daughter. If only Louis had not a wife already, and one whom he detested . . .

As soon as Louis XI was dead, Orléans began to develop his plans. He made overtures to the Duke of Brittany, his intermediary being William Chaumart, a monk of Fontevrault, the Abbey governed by Orléans' young sister. Shortly afterwards he slipped down the Loire to Nantes, and had an interview with Duke Francis. Meanwhile another emissary was sent to Rome, to set matters in train for an annulment of his marriage with Joan.

The conspiracy continued. Louis was now attempting to take over the regency from Anne de Beaujeu. The States General, summoned at Tours, refused to recognize his claim. He went on to Paris, stirring up trouble, trying to win support from the University and the civic authorities. Warning came, when he was in the middle of a game of tennis, that he was about to be arrested. He jumped on to a mule and disappeared from the city.

There was fighting: Louis, besieged in Beaugency, was forced to surrender and make his peace with the Regent.

Anne de Beaujeu, "La Grande" as she was called, was a woman of sterling character, intelligent, capable and wise. She was, in fact, the true daughter of Louis XI: " the least foolish of women," her father had boasted, qualifying the compliment by adding: "none of them have much sense." She was a match, at any rate, for Louis of Orléans. Her intelligence service was good, and she was well informed of his movements. Her competence preserved the crown for her young brother. Her kindness was the greatest support of her sister.

Joan had continued to live after marriage on the allowance her father made her. Orléans had always refused to touch the dowry and he had contributed nothing to her support. On one occasion only he made her a present of some pieces of gold, on the instigation, he afterwards declared, of his father-in-law. Now Anne came to the rescue, making her sister a suitable allowance and giving her an establishment at Amboise, in the part of the castle known as the Donjon. Here from time to time her husband joined her, generally when he was under suspicion, and wished to keep in favour with the ruling power.

He was, at this time, leading a gay and licentious life. Among his intimates he still maintained that he did not regard Joan as his wife; and he was renewing his intrigues with the Duke of Brittany. Anne de Beaujeu kept herself well informed of what was going on. She knew that his secret application to Rome for a declaration of Nullity had only been held up for a time by the death, in 1484, of Pope Sixtus IV. Orléans had opened up negotiations with the new Pope, Innocent VIII; but Anne, jealous for the honour of the royal house of France, used her influence to suppress the application.

In January 1487, Louis received a summons to wait upon the Regent Anne at Amboise. He pretended to obey; came so far, and then, under cover of a hunting expedition, made away in the opposite direction and never drew rein until he was safe across the border into Brittany. Here he became an active member of the party which was fighting for the independence of the duchy, always with a view to marriage with the heiress Anne of Brittany, a child of ten. There were two rivals in the field, Alain d'Albret, a powerful Gascon nobleman, and Maximilian of Austria, a widower of thirty-one, whose little daughter Margaret was betrothed to the young King of France.

A campaign of many months followed. The Regent entrusted the armies of France to a rising young commander, Louis de Trémoille, once the playmate of little Joan at Linières. Now, it was he who received in surrender the sword of her husband. Fighting desperately to the last, Louis was taken at St. Aubin-du-Cormier, and lodged in the castle of Sablé.

In the meantime, what of Joan? She had spent the last few months in a state of acute anxiety, torn by conflicting loyalties: the husband to whom she was bound, the sister whom she loved, ranged in opposite camps, angrily and bitterly opposed. When she heard the news of Louis' capture she set out at once to join him, escorted only by her equerry, La Palu. Louis had been transferred to Lusignan and there she found him, closely guarded, and none too tenderly treated by his gaoler. Louis gave her nothing but abuse; but his attitude changed somewhat when La Palu hinted that he might find her presence advantageous. Joan's first care was to get him removed to a better situation, her next, to work for his liberation.

Her efforts were seconded by such friends as Orléans

still maintained. These represented to him that he would do well to amend his attitude to his wife. She alone was in a position to effect anything in his favour. Marie of Clèves was dead, the Abbess of Fontevrault and her sister prudently kept out of the way. Anne de Beaujeu, tenderly as ever attached to her sister, and with a much clearer knowledge of his duplicity, was adamant. Orléans was a menace to the peace and security of the kingdom. He was safely under bolt and bar, and there he should remain.

Joan thereupon determined to appeal direct to the King. She followed him to Nantes, hoping to secure an interview. When she arrived, she found herself, as the wife of a declared traitor, suspect by all the Court. She could not even obtain a lodging. The story is told that she was wandering homeless about the city, attended only by La Palu and a few of her women, when she encountered the Captain of the Scottish Archers, and he, struck by her gentleness and her helpless situation, placed his own billet at her disposal.

Eventually Orléans was removed to the Great Tower of Bourges. This was a state prison of formidable aspect, dark and depressing. The duke had two rooms, scantily furnished, the chief article of furniture being a barred cage, kept always before his eyes as an awful warning of what he might expect. One of the rooms the duchess made over to her ladies, the other she shared with her husband. The place was barely habitable. Joan exerted herself, prevailed upon the municipality to provide the needful furnishings and cooking utensils, found a woman in Bourges to wash the old serge curtains, got the mattresses re-stuffed. She also succeeded in getting the harsh guard of Scottish Archers removed and their place taken by Frenchmen who treated the prisoner with less severity. She would stay a few days at a time, to see to her husband's wants and give him courage, and then be off again, travelling hither and thither, busy with his affairs.

The duke's property had been confiscated, and his household and servitors were suffering want. She relieved them out of her own purse, selling her plate and jewels for the purpose. When her funds were exhausted she wrote to du Bouchage to press for her allowance to be paid.

"I am applying to you," she wrote: "I am appealing to the King to be paid not only my allowance of the present year, but 2,000 livres owing from last year, and also 800 livres which I have not been able to recover from the Berry collectors; as the result of which I am in arrears to my treasurer to the amount of a good 3,000 livres, which I cannot pay unless I am allowed the said sums, for I have no other resources."

This appeal to the King was successful in its object. In the reply which Joan received it is stated in formal terms that her lack of money was due to "the great expense to which she has been and is daily put in pursuing the liberation of our said brother the Duke of Orléans." She was granted a sum of 4,000 livres "by favour of the great nearness of lineage in which she stands to Us . . . in consideration of our sister's humble supplication."

Then she remembered that Louis owned property in Italy which had escaped confiscation. His grandmother had been a Visconti and from her he had inherited Asti. Joan managed to get funds from here, and also to provide a delectable surprise. One day two mules from Italy came stepping into Bourges, bells tinkling upon their harness, laden with barrels of olive-oil and panniers containing oranges and jars of preserved fruits.

All this time Joan worked incessantly for her husband's release. She prayed, she interviewed, she wrote letters. The King was now of age, and beginning to take the government into his own hands. Anne de Beaujeu, on the death of her husband's brother, had become Duchess de Bourbon and was living in the Bourbon town of Moulins. She still remained a person of influence, and it was to her that Joan addressed her petition. The letter, couched and spelt in the quaint French of the period, has a direct, almost childlike appeal:

"My Sister,

"I am always appealing to you with great urgency, because I never cease to think of the deliverance of my lord husband. I have decided to put in writing the terms on which we may have peace and my husband freed, and I have written them to the King, and you will see it all. I entreat you to set your hand to this, so that these affairs may come to a happy conclusion, and you will make my husband and me your bondsmen for always. And for this I pray for you to God, that he may give you the perfection of your desires. Written at Saint-Martin-de-Gaude, this Tuesday evening.

"Sister, I beg you, put hand to it, that I may have an early answer.

"Your loving sister Jehanne de France."

Again she wrote:

"My Sister,

"I recommend myself right heartily to your remembrance in which I pray I may dwell, and do me the pleasure of often letting me have your news. It is my great misfortune that I no longer see you. Sister, I thank you for your litter which I am well pleased to have, and I should have done so before, but the man went off, and I did not know. Sister, touching the talk we had, you and I, all goes well. If it did not, I should have heard. I should have written to you long before this, but I thought you would take it for granted that the affairs I told you of were making progress. Sister, I beg you will urge on the matter of my husband and write to my brother about it, although he is acquitting himself well of the matter, for which we are truly bound to him and to you, my Sister, praying God that he will grant you what you desire.

"Your loving sister

"Jehanne de France."

At length her prayers were answered. One day in May 1491, after the Duke had been in prison for three years, the King rode to Bourges, stopping short of the town at the bridge of Baraugeon. Stuart of Aubigny was sent to bring out the prisoner. As they met, Orléans leapt from his horse and threw himself at the King's feet. Charles flung his arms round him, and there were tears on both sides. Then, bursting out laughing, they remounted their horses and rode into Bourges, where they feasted royally and ended up by sharing the one bed. Charles always had a great affection for his graceless brother-in-law.

"It was not owing to the representations of the Defendant that he was liberated," Louis had the ingratitude to depose later. "That was done by King Charles, and entirely on his own accord."

Restored to freedom and to the enjoyment of his estates, the Duke of Orléans seemed to turn over a new leaf. Even his wife was sensible of the change in his demeanour. He arranged for her to have a triumphal entry into the city of Orléans and contributed 500 livres towards the expenses. It was a great occasion. All the gentry in the town and the whole population turned out to greet her, as with church bells pealing and crowds cheering wildly she was borne in on her chair, splendidly dressed in cloth of gold, a canopy held over her head by four of the principal nobles. The Duke was not beside her. He had made his state entry already.

They were together, however, on many occasions; at Tours, at Blois, Amboise, Paris. Now at last they seemed to be entering into a new life.

So great was the favour which the Duke of Orléans enjoyed at this time, that he was entrusted with the negotiations for the marriage of the King with that same princess whom he had formerly coveted for himself, Anne of Brittany. Charles' armies had overrun Brittany and Duke Francis was dead. The young duchess had been married to Maximilian, but only by proxy, and Maximilian had not yet claimed his bride. The delay was his undoing. Charles broke off his engagement to Maximilian's daughter and secured the heiress of Brittany for himself. The marriage took place at Langeais, on December the 6th, 1491, and little Princess Margaret was returned, disappointed, to her father.

Orléans took an active part in the marriage. He had a secret satisfaction at seeing a certain clause inserted in the contract. It stipulated that, should Charles VIII die without issue, the Duchess Anne should espouse his heir: that is to say, Orléans himself, provided he were free to marry. Such a contingency, however, appeared remote when, the following year, Anne of Brittany gave birth to a son.

The child was christened Charles Orland, or Roland, after the somewhat romantic notions of his father, and he was held at the font by the venerable Francis of Paola. The saintly old man, who came to Plessis to attend the deathbed of Louis XI, had received from him the special charge of watching over his children. After the death of Louis, Francis remained in France, faithfully fulfilling the task he had undertaken. From him Joan received much consolation and support during those harrowing years.

Charles VIII, thirsting for adventure, elected to pursue the claim to the kingdom of Naples which he derived from his grandmother, Yolande of Anjou.

He collected a formidable army and advanced into Italy. Louis went with the expedition as far as his own town of Asti, and there remained, while Charles pushed his way on towards Naples. It is unnecessary to recount the details of this campaign, which, brilliant at its commencement, was only saved from disaster by the French victory at Fornova, where a remnant of the expeditionary force succeeded in cutting their way back to France.

During the months of war, Joan and the Queen made Lyons their headquarters and there waited anxiously for news of their husbands. Anne of Bourbon was again in charge of the kingdom, Joan of Orléans had the care of her husband's duchy. She was incessantly on the move, from Blois to Plessis, from Plessis to Montrichard and back again to Lyons, watching over her husband's interests, seeing to the needs of his people; then on her knees, praying for his safety.

Word came from Italy that the duke was ill. Soloman de Bombelles, his physician, was concerned about his condition, and desired another opinion, that of the monk-doctor, John Bourgeois. No one knew where he was. Joan sent out horsemen in all directions until he was found, and made arrangements for his speedy transport into Italy. For this she received a letter of thanks. "Madame m'amye," it began, and ended up "Vostre amy," "Your *friend*," not "Your *husband*."

When he returned, they resumed life together. They appeared at Blois, Amboise, Montrichard. Whether or not as the result of their fruitless expedition, both he and Charles seemed to have learned wisdom and sobriety. Then came an event which brought sorrow to the one and secret elation to the other. One month after their triumphal return, in December 1495, the Dauphin, a fine little lad of three, brimming with life and utterly fearless, was suddenly taken ill and died in a few hours. Tragedy after tragedy followed. Three years in succession Anne bore her husband children, only to lose them after the briefest span of life.

Louis of Orléans watched events as a gambler might watch the fall of the dice. Stronger and stronger grew his chances; but he was getting impatient. He had resumed his careless, licentious ways of living, and now he fell under suspicion of mismanaging affairs in Normandy, the duchy granted him by Charles VIII, and plotting against the royal authority. The affair was growing serious, and once again he found it convenient to take shelter with his wife at Montilz-les-Blois. He was there with her when a courier came galloping in, bringing news which was to have a profound effect upon the future of both of them: on the Eve of Palm Sunday 1498, after an illness lasting only an hour or two, Charles VIII had breathed his last.

Joan's husband was King of France.

CHAPTER VI

A QUEEN WITHOUT A CROWN

SO rapid has been the march of events during the last few years that we have almost lost sight of Joan. What kind of woman was she at this juncture of her life, when she became, with such tragic suddenness, Queen of France?

The silent, prayerful child of Linières was now a woman of thirty-four. Her character, deeply rooted in piety and the love of God, had matured. She had grown more thoughtful, more patient, more loyal. The luxury and easy morals of the times in which she lived had not sullied her purity. All the pains and disillusions which life had brought her had not abated her charity. She had become a great lady, capable, energetic, resourceful, competent to rule. She had all the makings of a queen; all, that is, except two: she lacked physical beauty, and she was childless.

The woman whose delicate constitution we noted in the days when Louis her father placed her in the quiet country surroundings of Linières, still bore in her body the traces of that early complaint. She was short and awkward in figure. The golden glory had faded from her hair. Only the lovely eyes maintained their beauty, tender to plead in charity, quick to flash in righteous indignation.

She was not by any means a cripple or helpless. We have seen how she travelled up and down France during the months when her husband was in prison or abroad, and all his affairs depended upon her energetic administration. In her day, travel was no easy adventure ; it was a matter of physical discomfort and weariness. We do not know whether she rode. There seems to be no mention in her life of horsemanship; possibly she was not able. Her journeys were made in her litter, a sort of carriage slung from poles and borne between two horses or mules: it was the normal means of transport for a lady of her rank. In this fashion she would swing along the dusty bridle-paths and splash through the streams. There was little ease and comfort in the task that Joan undertook when she managed the duchy of Orléans.

So much of her life we know only through the smoked distorting glass of the Interrogations that we are glad to turn to speculation in order to fill up the gaps. Where, for instance, did she get her knowledge of cookery ? We shall see her, before long, lifting the saucepan-lids in the kitchen of the Annonciade, and discussing ways of serving eggs. Was she recalling things which an observant little girl had noted when, free from restraints of etiquette, she had loved to linger in the great kitchen at Linières ? Or had necessity taught her to cope with a charcoal brazier or a smoking wood-fire in an attempt to turn out something which would tempt the appetite of a surly, thankless man held close in the Great Tower of Bourges?

Louis XII was crowned at Rheims. On July the 2nd he made his state entry into Paris. Joan was not present on either occasion.

It may be that the omission did not trouble her unduly. The coronation of a King of France was a ceremony almost sacramental. It concerned the person of the King and him alone. Louis XI, as we have seen, did not wait for his wife to be present at his coronation. So it is possible that even now Joan may not have known of the thing that the King had in mind. She may still have been ignorant of the fact that Louis' first action on his succession had been to despatch an envoy to Rome, asking for a speedy pronouncement of nullity and for the dispensation necessary to allow him to marry his cousin's widow, Anne of Brittany.

Alexander VI, who then occupied the Papal throne, is possibly the least reputable of all the Popes who ever filled the See of Peter. A Spaniard, a member of the family of Borgia, he was luxurious, ambitious, unscrupulous. He had a family to make provision for, born, be it said in all justice, before his accession to the Papal Chair. His favourite son, Caesar Borgia, Cardinal-Archbishop of Valencia, was anxious to resign the ecclesiastical state and enter upon a career in the world. The Pope desired, of all things, the creation of a duchy for this son of his in the fair kingdom of France.

Let it be stated here, however, that though Alexander VI had every reason to conciliate and favour the King of France, he made no attempt to interfere with the customary procedure of the Court. One assistance he could give : he had the nominating of the Commissioners. But those whom he did nominate, though friendly to the King, do not seem to have abused their position. Further than this the Pope would not go. Indeed, as he wrote to Louis in the middle of the Process, any attempt to overrule the proceedings would simply be to play into the hands of the opposition. Let the law take its course.

One day Joan received a visitor. It was Louis de Trémoille. He had made his peace with the King, who observed magnanimously: "The King of France does not revenge the injuries done to the Duke of Orléans." Now he came to Joan, courteous, possibly unwilling, but nevertheless the bearer of the King's communication. It was charmingly put. "Madame, the King commends himself to you, and has charged me to say that the lady in all the world whom he holds most dear is yourself, his next of kin, for the graces and virtues which you display, and he is truly grieved that you are not disposed to have issue, for he would dearly love to end his days in a companionship so holy as yours." He went on to suggest that the marriage—which was no marriage—should terminate, in order that the King might be free to seek a wife elsewhere.

According to Jean Bouchet, who relates this incident, Joan's reply was: "Were I convinced that there was no lawful marriage between the King and me, I should beg him in all affection to let me live in perpetual chastity; for my chief desire is to live for ever with the Eternal King, despising the honours of the world and the joys of the flesh."

The honours of the world. . . . She was, it is true, a King's daughter. She had known pomp and state, court etiquette, lip service. She had known other things, too: the pain of sitting neglected and humiliated at the banquet-table, the slights, the smiles, the innuendoes of her husband's fashionable companions. She had breathed the sickening atmosphere of court intrigue, tasted the agonising anxiety of a wife whose husband's escapades rendered him always untrustworthy and frequently brought him into peril of his life. She, who from birth had been one of the first ladies of the land, had felt the sting of poverty, known its physical discomfort, and mental distress.

The joys of the flesh. . . . She had given herself, in filial obedience, to a man who abhorred her and who made no secret of his abhorrence. She had yielded him her maidenhood; and her marriage had been joyless and sterile. She was childless. We know, from occasional words that she let fall, what that meant to her, how she regretted it.

The honours of the world, the joys of the flesh: how gladly would she give them up! how readily would she despise them, if only she "were convinced that there was no marriage between the King and her." But she was not so convinced.

With all that was at stake, with a prospect of relief from the wearying, humiliating yoke which bound her to this man who hated her, she still held fast to what she believed to be true: "I am his wife."

It was perhaps the greatest temptation of her life.

We shall see her in court, confronted with incident after incident of her husband's repudiation of her, holding fast to her position: "I am his wife." One little admission made, one single doubt taken advantage of, might have contributed to break the bond which must have been as distasteful to her as it was to him. She did not permit herself to take it. She was his wife.

A marriage made by God is for life, and only death can dissolve it. Joan believed in the validity of her marriage, and she was prepared to defend her belief to the utmost of her power. It was for the Holy See to determine whether the union into which she had entered twenty-two years previously was a true marriage in the sight of God, or whether, owing to some flaw present at the time of the union, no marriage had ever taken place. This is the meaning of a declaration of nullity, a totally different thing from the process known as divorce, in which it is assumed that a marriage, duly performed and consummated, may be dissolved as the result of circumstances arising afterwards, an attitude never tolerated by the Catholic Church.

The case opened at Tours on August the 9th, only twelve days after the issuing of the Bull which constituted proceedings. Two commissioners were appointed. One was Fernand of Almeida, Bishop of Ceuta and Papal Nuncio to France. He was a Portuguese, and his direction of the case, if unbiased, was unhelpful. Six weeks later he was replaced as President of the Court by Philip of Luxembourg,

Bishop of Mans, an old friend and fellow-conspirator of Louis of Orléans. The Bishop of Ceuta then retired from the bench, but remained in court, an interested spectator.

The other commissioner was the Bishop of Albi, Louis of Amboise, a member of the noble family of Chaumont-Amboise, which produced many notable men and women and gave many sons to the Church. George of Amboise, his brother, was destined to be Louis XII's chief minister and to render great services to France. One of the stipulations in the alliance between Pope and King was a Cardinal's hat for George of Amboise. Louis of Amboise, however, had the happy knack of being on friendly terms with all parties. He had served Louis XI, he had kept the favour of both the house of Orléans and that of France, and he was to prove a sincere and kind friend to Joan in and after her tribulation.

She needed a friend. She found herself now, at this crisis of her life, utterly alone. Her brother was dead. Her sister was powerless to help her. The husband who had sworn to be her protector was her chief opponent. And he had the means to make himself obeyed. At his bidding every person who could recall any circumstance which might be twisted to Joan's discredit was summoned to come and give evidence. There were over forty of these. Joan for her part with difficulty found four, all reluctant and unhelpful.

The King could command the best legal opinion. The first advocates in the land were proud to conduct his case. No one was anxious to represent Joan. Of the four barristers appointed her, only two, Mark

Travers and Francis Bethoulat, the latter under protest, could be found to carry on. Halfway through the action the court made an order, backed by a threat of excommunication, for some of the legal faculty of Bourges to come and advise her. Of the four summoned only one appeared, and he demanded a safe conduct in writing as a precaution against possible reprisals.

On August 30th Joan appeared in answer to the citation, to receive the counts upon which the declaration of nullity was sought. These were four in number: the blood-relationship between the contracting parties, their spiritual relationship, the violence and intimidation to which the King had been subjected at the time of the marriage, and the incapacity of the Queen to perform the act of marriage. A week later she announced her intention of contesting each point, and on September the 13th, at one o'clock in the afternoon, she underwent her first interrogation in the house of the Dean at Tours. Statements had been prepared in advance, requiring as answer a simple affirmative or negative: "I agree," or "I do not think so."

"Did she know," Joan was asked, "that the King had yielded only to terrible threats on the part of Louis XI, such as the threat of losing all his possessions, or being put to death by drowning?"

"She did not believe it: had never heard of such a thing."

"Had the King never told her of these threats?"

"No."

"Had he never complained to other people?"

"She did not know."

"Had no one else ever mentioned these complaints to her?"

"No."

"Did she know that her father King Louis had a way of dealing with disobedient subjects and treating them cruelly?"

"She did not believe it." She had known very little of her father, in fact.

"Did she know that threats of this kind had forced the young Louis into a pretended marriage with her, and that he had often protested against the violence and fear to which he had been subjected?"

"She did not."

"Did she know that after the death of Louis XI the Duke had made no secret of his wishes and of his repudiation of the marriage?"

"She did not know it, and she did not believe it."

Pressed on this point, "she did not know it, and had never heard of it."

They took her through the campaign in Brittany, trying to get her to admit that Louis' actions had been instigated throughout with the sole object of contracting a fresh marriage.

"She did not know it, and she did not believe it."

"Did she not know that this was the cause of Louis' having been detained in prison in various places?"

"She knew nothing of the cause of his detention."

"Did she not know that a prisoner suffered from considerable discomfort?"

"She did know it."

"Did she not know that he was treated with great severity by some of his gaolers?"

"She knew it only too well."

"Did she not know that it was for this reason that he had been obliged to keep up the deception until after the death of King Charles VIII?"

"She did not believe it."

Her answers were made quietly and firmly. They went on to the fourth impeachment.

"Did she know that she was not as well formed as most women?"

"Yes, she knew it." There was no pride or resentment in her voice, though the question must have hurt.

"Did she know that she was incapable of bearing children, or of performing the marriage act?"

She answered firmly and with a flash of spirit: "I do not believe it."

After this interrogation she submitted to the tribunal the following letter:

"My Lords, I am a woman, ignorant of procedure, and I find the present affair most distasteful. I beg you to bear with me if I make any statement or answer which is not what it should be. And I protest that, if in my answers I refer to any matter upon which I am not questioned, or which my Lord the King has not included in his indictment, it shall not be taken to my prejudice, or to the advantage of my Lord the King. I adhere to my request for the greatest possible expedition: and I never thought that this matter would come to an action between my Lord the King and me. I ask, my Lords, that this protest may be included in the process."

D'Estang, the King's counsel, put in a demand that the physical condition of the Queen should be examined into and reported upon by competent women. She asked time to consider the matter.

The court then proceeded to examine the witnesses. An epidemic breaking out in Tours obliged the tribunal to remove to Amboise. There, one after another, they came to give their evidence: ancient followers of the house of Orléans, de Vatan, with twenty-six years of service, son of the King's governor: de Rabaudanges, reputed to be his step-father: Gaillard, his treasurer: members of his council as Duke, Bertrand, de Symphorien, de Gié and a host of others: the clerics, Canon Chardon his chaplain, Canon Calipel his secretary, and Chaumart, the Augustinian monk who had been his envoy to Rome. There were the great ladies of the Court of Blois, sweeping in with their rustling silks and jewelled head-dresses, Elisabeth Fricon, Vatan's sister, who had been maid-of-honour to Marie of Clèves, and had been present at the King's christening and also at his wedding. She deposed to the savage character of Louis XI, the reluctant attitude of the young bridegroom, the many discussions which had taken place among him and his friends with regard to the action to be taken to rid him of an unwelcome bride: the other ladies, Martine de Dampierre and Marie de Marcilly, supporting her statements. There were the two nuns, Perrette de Cambray and Louise Jarry, to bear witness to Joan's unfortunate deformity and the abhorrence with which the duke regarded her. There were these and many others.

Slowly, surely, D'Estang built up the case for intimidation. Day after day, as autumn closed in and the court grew darker and colder, the Cardinal and the Bishops sat and listened to the witnesses, the notaries pegging away after them, taking down every word in long-hand, sitting on at the end of the session to render the whole into crabbed and villainous Latin. It is from their records and the stories they contain, true or false as they may be, that we derive our knowledge of Joan's unhappy married life.

She was not present at these interrogations. Her personal secretary, Charles de Preux, acted for her and reported on each day's doings. She had known, it is true, that her husband disliked her; he had made no secret of that; but she had not known—so she deposed upon oath, and we believe her—of the violent pressure put upon him before and after marriage, and of his attempts to free himself. Now she learns the story, relentlessly unrolling, of what lay behind her marriage, of incident after incident compelling him, culminating in a terrible scene with Louis XI, related by de Castelnau, in which the duke was threatened that if he did not go at once to Linières and comport himself as a husband, the King would have him thrown into the river. And it was no idle threat. D'Estang brought witnesses to show that, in matters of this kind, Louis XI was a man of his word.

The tale went on. The depositions described

Orléans' compulsory visits to Joan at Linières and elsewhere, the disdain with which he treated her, the pretences he kept up in order to deceive the spies with which he was surrounded. They disclosed the intrigues with Brittany, the move to obtain a declaration of nullity so as to be free to marry the heiress Anne. They ascribed to the restless and frustrated life of the duke: all his disloyalty, his rebellions, resulting in the imprisonment which had so broken his spirit as to make him incapable of offering further resistance.

A marriage is a free contract between two persons who are capable of entering into it. If one of the parties is under the influence of a fear which is grave, is produced by some person other than himself (or herself), is unjust, and offers no alternative but marriage, and if under these circumstances the marriage ceremony is performed, since that person is not a free agent, no marriage can take place: the marriage is null. Such a marriage may, however, be rectified by the subsequent free consent of both parties. The Canon law of the time ruled that if, the cause of fear having been removed and a reasonable time having elapsed, the party who had suffered constraint continued to cohabit and took no steps to seek a declaration of nullity, he or she might be assumed to have given free consent and thereby validated the marriage.

The attitude taken by the defence was that there had been several periods during which Orléans was free from constraint and might have claimed his liberty, and he had not done so. The witnesses had established that during these periods he had cohabited with Joan on various occasions, and it was claimed that he had thereby "purged his fear," and made his marriage valid. He on the other hand maintained that no matter when he had lived with her, it was *always* under the influence of fear: fear of offending Louis XI, fear of the Regent Anne and of Charles VIII, fear of losing life or possessions, fear of imprisonment, of a lifetime of constraint.

Meanwhile D'Estang had not lost sight of the fourth impeachment, that of incapacity for marriage. It was claimed that Joan was so ill formed from childhood as to be unable to perform the marriage act.

This was a difficult and delicate matter to establish, but Canon law recognised several ways in which it might be done. There was the physical examination by experts of the party alleged to be impotent: there were the depositions of witnesses, and the sworn statement of the party maintaining the validity of the marriage. It was left to the option of the judges to decide which method or methods should be adopted in any particular case.

Repeatedly the King's counsel demanded that Joan should submit to a physical examination. Such a course was repugnant to her. In a letter which she submitted to the tribunal, she suggested instead that the King be challenged to speak on oath of the relations between them, and "begs him very humbly, as her Lord, that he will not take it ill of her that she should decline to permit a thing which would lessen her estate, an estate all too low with regard to the house from which she is sprung."

On October the 26th Bethoulat summed up the case for the Queen. It was a statement which covered the whole of her married life, from her wedding-day down to the death of Charles VIII. It alleged that the marriage, if null at the outset, had been ratified by subsequent free consent; it denied the charge of impotence, and referred to the many occasions on which, according to the Defendant's deposition, the marriage had been consummated.

The King answered these statements in person. On October the 29th the two commissioners, and de Preux, the Queen's representative, waited upon him at Madan. His attitude was a simple denial of everything. He had never done it: or if he had, it was because he was *afraid*. He had never *voluntarily* acknowledged her as his wife, never given her anything, never accepted anything from her. Some of his statements did him little credit. He contradicted himself, vaunted his own duplicity and mendacity in Brittany, admitted that, for his own safety and security, he had prolonged a situation that was sinful in itself if he did not consider himself to be married; but his statements agreed with the depositions of his witnesses.

It looks as though the case for intimidation was fully established, and with this the whole process might have been brought to an end; but, possibly in respect for the memory of Louis XI, the tribunal decided to deal also with the indictment of impotence.

The case began to drag, and the King was growing impatient. He had good reason for his anxiety. His contract with Anne of Brittany stipulated that the marriage was to take place within the year, and in the meantime she had gone back to Brittany, sadly grieving for the young husband she had lost. Moreover, there was evidence of a rising tide of indignation on the Queen's behalf. The theologians whom Louis consulted were not quite unanimous in his favour. John Stanbrouk, member of the Sorbonne, made open protest, and later on the popular preacher, the Franciscan Oliver Maillard, denounced the action of the King from the pulpit.

On November the 20th, with the effect of a thunderbolt, a fresh piece of evidence was put in. This was the famous letter, already quoted, written by Louis XI to Dammartin, referring to the marriage of his daughter, in which he stated: "I have decided to go on with the marriage of my little daughter Joan with the little Duke of Orléans, because I fancy that the children they will have together will not cost them much to rear. I advise you that I mean to accomplish this marriage, elsewise those who go contrary to me will have no assurance of life in my Realm."

Much has been written concerning this letter. Its production at this particular juncture has tended to throw doubt upon its authenticity, but the experts then and now regard it as authentic, and indeed there is evidence, in a letter written by Charles VIII to Dammartin, that the former knew of the existence of this dangerous document and was attempting to get possession of it. Moreover, an explanation was given, a reason why it had not been produced earlier in the Process. It was in the keeping of Dammartin's son, John de Chabannes, whose wife Susanne was the daughter of Joan's half-sister, another Joan, the widow of the Admiral de Bourbon. It was produced together with a note from the latter lady begging Chabannes to keep it out of court. She was evidently unwilling to see published a document harmful alike to her father's memory and her sister's cause.

This document was seized upon with eagerness as establishing the count of sterility. Louis had foreseen that his daughter would be childless. He had in fact married her to the Duke of Orléans *for that very reason,* hoping thereby to extinguish the house of Orléans. A little consideration will show that, in the case of a child of twelve years or less, such a conclusion could not possibly be drawn. Louis might have had a suspicion that his daughter would not bear children, or that her children might not be healthy. He could not possibly have had any certainty. The letter strengthened the case for intimidation at the time of the marriage; but it was on the final count, that of incapacity, that the King's counsel was anxious to establish a decision.

On November the 24th another letter was received from the Queen. She expressed her willingness to abide by the good faith of the court and the King's statement on oath with regard to the nature of the relations between them.

The King consented to undergo a second interrogation, and engaged to receive the commissioners at Dudau on the Loire, on December the 4th. When they arrived they found he was no longer there. A flood had obliged him to remove to Ligueil. Here, on the following day, he made his statement.

He was warned of the solemnity of the oath he was taking: "The act of a true King, as is the Claimant, is to fear God and to speak the truth, following in the way of Jesus Christ himself, our Creator, who is the very Truth: and if he speak the truth, he will be prosperous in God, and will obtain an inestimable treasure, that is to say, Paradise: but if he do the contrary, he will be labouring unto Hell. . . ."

Then he proceeded to deny every one of Joan's assertions. He had never been agreeable, for instance, to her visits at Lusignan or Bourges. She had had nothing to do with his liberation from prison.

He had never *willingly* received her as his wife. He had tried, under compulsion, to conduct himself towards her as a husband should, but he could never succeed. He had made strenuous efforts on various occasions, but he had never been able to do it.

This was the oath which brought the long case to an end. It was something more than the sworn statement of a husband: ordinarily that might be accepted only from the party who was *maintaining* the validity of the marriage. It was the honour of a King, the oath of one who knew no superior, was responsible to no other. "The King can do no wrong." The Queen had claimed it and the King had given it.

A few days later her counsel submitted a note in which she accepted the King's declaration.

The findings of the Commission were promulgated shortly afterwards: "By our considered decision, which we have taken, sitting in judgment, having before our eyes God alone, from the mouth of Whom, seated upon His throne, proceedeth the two-edged sword, by that decision herein contained, we do state, declare and pronounce that the marriage contracted between the parties, the validity of which has been in question in this action, has not existed and does not exist, but has been and is null and without validity, obligation or efficacy: nothing hinders the lord Claimant from contracting a marriage with another woman. By virtue of the Apostolic authority we accord to him the faculty for this in so far as it is necessary, by reason of the causes, pleas and reasonings declared in the Process. We declare the lady Defendant absolved of all charges and liabilities."

What conclusions are we to draw from this?

First, that on the evidence submitted, the court could have come to no other decision. No reasons are given; but the fact that the King alone was granted permission to marry, nothing being said about Joan, seems to indicate that the commissioners judged her incapable of marriage. This, in view of the King's sworn statement and her own refusal to submit to a physical examination, is understandable.

What is the truth of the matter? Unless we assume that Louis XII and his witnesses perjured themselves from beginning to end—a view taken by some of Joan's biographers—we are driven to conclude that she was honestly and genuinely in error in believing that the relations between Louis and herself were those of normal, satisfying marriage. We cannot doubt, from our knowledge of her character and integrity, that the statement she made was the truth as far as she knew it.

The findings of the court were published on

December the 17th. Two days earlier Joan received a private communication. The Bishop of Albi waited on her, accompanied by one who was henceforth to be her greatest friend. This was the Franciscan, Gilbert Nicholas, better known by the name which he later received, Gabriel-Maria.

It was the latter who addressed her. He was carrying the fateful parchment concealed in the sleeve of his habit. "Madame," he said, "these sleeves of mine are filled with patience for sale: would you care to buy some? It is a commodity of which you have need."

She understood him instantly. "I am no longer Queen of France," she said: and then the tears came freely.

"God be praised," she said at last: "I know he has permitted this to happen in order to detach me from the world, and give me the means of serving him better than I have done hitherto."

She was quite composed when she attended the Church of St. Denys at Amboise to hear the public reading of the decree. It was a bright, clear day, only a week before Christmas. The church was packed. Clergy, nobles, tradesmen and working folk, the curious, the sympathetic, the lovers of sensation, all were there. A high chair, covered with crimson velvet starred with fleurs-de-lys, was placed ready for her. There seated, in the sight of all, she awaited the reading of her sentence.

The Cardinal of Luxembourg stood up, the parchment in his hand, and began to read. His voice was faint and did not carry. People craned their heads forward to hear. All at once the church began to grow very dark. Torches had to be brought, and it was by the light of these, interrupted by flashes of lightning and rolls of thunder, that the Cardinal proceeded to read to the end. There were murmurs of indignation as he finished. As the procession passed out, angry mutterings could be heard: "Caiaphas! Annas!" and again: "Pilate! Herod!"

The King was not present. He was keeping well out of the way, and he had a rather important engagement at this time. Ever since November the 7th Caesar Borgia had been waiting at Valence, the seat of his new duchy, waiting to receive his investiture and to hand over to the King a document which he had brought with him—the dispensation for the marriage of Louis to Anne of Brittany. On December the 19th he and the King met at Chinon. He made a splendid entry. There were seventy mules carrying his baggage, sixteen chargers with trappings of silver and cloth of gold, pages, musicians, a great suite of attendants: last came Borgia himself, costumed in crimson satin and cloth of gold, stiff with jewels from head to foot.

Render to Caesar the things that are Caesar's . . . Caesar got them all: the duchy of Valence, with 100,000 livres paid down for the acquisition of land, the pension of 20,000 livres, the company of men-at-arms, the princess whom Louis had undertaken to find him for wife.[1] The lady was Charlotte d'Albret, daughter of that d'Albret who had formerly made suit for the hand of Anne of Brittany. After a brief honeymoon

[1] Borgia had, by special dispensation, received permission to marry.

her husband left her and she never saw him again. It was at the court of Joan of France that she found consolation, and it was under Joan's protection that her little daughter was born.

. . . *and to God the things that are God's*: "Praise be to God," Joan said: "he has permitted this in order to give me the means of serving him better."

CHAPTER VII

DUCHESS OF BERRY

LOUIS XII showed himself more kindly disposed towards his "dear and well-beloved cousin" than he had ever been towards his wife. The deed making provision for her was issued at Loudun and dated the 26th December, 1498. After a reference to the opposition he had always maintained to the marriage contracted in his minority, and the pronouncement of the Church concerning its nullity, the King went on to say: "Wherefore we deem it right and seemly that we, who by the grace of God have succeeded to the crown of France, through the deaths in succession of our cousins Louis and Charles, of whom our cousin is daughter and sister, should have regard to the provision and entreatment of her and her estate after a manner which befits and pertains to her as daughter and sister of Kings of France."

He made over to her the principality of Berry, with all emoluments, "making and creating our said cousin Duchess of the said duchy, with the enjoyment for her lifetime only of all sovereign rights, honours, prerogatives, pre-eminences and jurisdictions." He reserved to himself the right to homage, and the royal privileges connected with ecclesiastical foundations; but she was to have an annual allowance of 30,000 francs and the income accruing from certain cities and commercial undertakings. On January the 8th, exactly three weeks after the promulgation of the decree of nullity, Louis XII was married to Anne of Britanny and passed out of the life of Joan of France.

Not entirely: she continued to wear her wedding-ring. There was that frail link between them still. There was also the loyalty of a daughter of France towards the one who personified her country. Every day she prayed for the good estate of "Alexander our Pope and Louis our King," and she prayed sincerely and with a full heart.

The ordeal through which she had passed affected her deeply. It was a full year, the chronicler of the Annonciade tells us, before she got over it. "When she was at meat, she would be quite distrait, and the pallor of her countenance was such that it might have been covered with earth."

In a book of Hours, preserved in the *Bibliothèque de l'Arsenal*, there is a miniature portrait which has been identified with Joan of France. It represents her kneeling at a prie-dieu, her hands folded in prayer. She is wearing a rich dress of crimson, the long wide sleeves turned back to show a lining of white: on her head is a veil flowing over her shoulders almost to the ground. The features, alert, composed, bear sufficient resemblance to those of the death-mask to make identification probable. This is further supported by the royal arms, the shield of fleurs-de-lys of gold upon a field of azure, and the crown, surmounting the picture; also by the monogram I.M., which stands for Jehanne Marienne (Joan of Mary), the name she adopted in her latter years. There is no suggestion in this portrait of any physical abnormality. Possibly the artist wished to flatter; on the other hand, such a picture tends to render unlikely any such gross deformity as some of her biographers have depicted.

On February the 10th, 1499, Joan did homage for her duchy, not to the King in person, but to his delegate. Peter de Rohan, Marshal de Gié, was the person deputed to represent the King. He had been one of the witnesses in the Process, and on oath had made particularly unpleasant statements about her; now it was he who received her oath of loyalty. Shortly afterwards, the new Duchess of Berry issued a letter to her subjects:

"On behalf of the Duchess of Berry.

"Most dear and well-beloved, it has pleased the King to bestow upon us the duchy of Berry, together with other domains and manors as contained in his letters patent ratified by his Houses of Parliament and his Treasury at Paris, and to put us in possession he has made order in writing to the Archdeacon de Refuge, one of his councillors in the said Parliament, who goes at our request to the said Bourges, to take delivery and enter into possession on our behalf. Wherefore we beg that you will give diligent heed to the enactment of the said Refuge in such a way as to afford us matter for contentment with you. Moreover we would have you harken to our well-beloved and faithful steward Guichard de Vauxrion, whom we have charged to converse to you of other matters, and to have confidence in his words. Very dear and beloved friends, may our Lord have you in his keeping. Written at Amboise the 17th day of February.

"Jehanne de France."

The Duchess arrived in person on the evening of the 12th of March, and rested for the night at the Benedictine Abbey of St. Sulpice. The following day she made her entry into Bourges. Her first halt was at the Cathedral of St. Stephen, and she visited the Sainte Chapelle before taking possession of her new home, the Royal Lodge.

Bourges, the principal city of Berry, had been familiar to Joan in childhood, when she was accustomed to have periods of residence there with the de Linières. It was then a fair and prosperous city. Now all was changed. A devastating fire in the year 1487 had burnt out more than half the city, and destroyed most of the public buildings and upwards of seven thousand homes. Many of the inhabitants had left the town and sought a living elsewhere. Trade was languishing and there was evidence of want on all sides. Fortunately the cathedral had escaped destruction, and so had the Royal Lodge and its adjoining chapel.

Little remains to-day of this palace, built at enormous expense by John the Magnificent, 1st Duke of Berry. It was not a beautiful building, being constructed for strength rather than elegance; but, though heavy and ill lighted, the interior was rich and sumptuously furnished. The chapel attached to the palace was built by the same Duke John, in imitation of the Sainte Chapelle of St. Louis at Paris, which it even surpassed in beauty of design and decoration. It housed some precious relics, including three thorns from the Sacred Crown. Nothing of this beautiful church remains. It was badly damaged by fire, and in 1756 its destruction was completed by a storm, after which it was demolished.

There was another building nearby, the sight of which would have brought a pang to Joan's heart: the Great Tower, that dark prison where she had spent so many anxious hours. It was one of the first places she visited as she made her entry, borne on her litter through the cheering crowds. She found prisoners languishing there, and to all but the worst she gave their liberty, pardoning their offences in honour of the occasion.

There were others among the crowd acclaiming her who needed, and obtained, her forgiveness: the lawyers who had failed her in her need, the men who had defamed her and given false witness. She had no thought of retaliation. She desired only to forget the past and enter upon her reign here in the hearts of her people; and it was not long before they began to realise it, and to appreciate her worth.

Wisely and carefully she chose her ministers. In charge of administration she placed Peter d'Aumont, a man of ability and future Marshal of France. Vincent de Puy, a member of the Vatan family, some of whom had shown her little friendship in her recent trial, she made her bailiff. Bien-aimé George de Mannay, "Well-beloved George," was her equerry, her right-hand man in all practical concerns. The Bishop of Autun, Louis of Amboise, a nephew of the bishop who had been her judge, she made her chief Almoner. He grew to be her very good friend, and to hold her in the highest esteem. In addition to the ordinary ministers of State, she appointed an inner circle of personal advisers. These were: the above-mentioned Bishop of Autun; William of Cambrai, Archbishop of Bourges; Guy Juvenal, Abbot of St. Sulpice; Gilbert Nicholas, her confessor; and George Passerin, her chaplain.

She had her little court of women, too, carefully chosen for their virtue and discretion: Madame d'Aumont, the wife of her chief minister; Joan de Graville, Madame de Chaumont, the wife of yet another member of the Chaumont-Amboise family; Charlotte d'Albret, the forsaken wife of Caesar Borgia; and Charlotte de Bourbon, Countess de Nevers. Marie Pot was her lady-in-waiting, and she had two young maids-of-honour, whom she held in great affection, Frances de Mohet and Joan de Bourbon.

Under such auspices there was good government. A woman of courage, prudence and energy, with a heart full of the love of God, and with charity towards all men ruling her conduct, can accomplish great things both in public and in private life. The Duchess of Berry was successful in both. Of her private life we shall see more hereafter. Of the work which she accomplished for her people we know this, and it means much: she speedily acquired, and retained, the title of "the Good Duchess."

Unfortunately, during the civil wars of Religion which broke out only a few years later, the city archives, from which we might have learned some details regarding her methods of administration, were lost. An incident, however, which occurred twenty years after her death, gives some indication. At that time another princess, Margaret of Angoulême, sister of King Francis I, was taking up the reins of government in Berry. She wished to alter the judicial system, to establish Courts of Assize such as were being set up in other parts of France. The people of Bourges were unanimous in asking that no change should be made. They had the system introduced by "the Good Duchess," and it was good enough for them. They desired nothing better. A hundred years after her death her memory was still green, when the citizens of Bourges gave testimony to "the temporal benefits conferred in days of old, which by her bounty adorned her duchy of Berry."

She found much in Bourges to excite her compassion. There were poverty and distress, and these she set herself to relieve. Hers was not an indiscriminate giving of alms, but an organised system of relief, founded upon the charity of Christ. She understood the pride that made acceptance difficult, and the ladies to whom she entrusted this work of love were instructed to make the most delicate enquiries and to treat with absolute discretion and secrecy the needs they uncovered.

She had an especial pity for the unfortunates of her own sex: the "poor daughters of joy," she tenderly called them. Every means was tried to raise them from misery: entreaties, words of love, gifts of money, marriage dowries. Little by little they would be lifted up and set upon their feet.

Sick people she would visit in person, and see to their needs, feeding and washing them, dressing their sores. When the Process for her Beatification opened in 1515, evidence was given regarding her charity by Friar Ambrose Basset.

"I have heard tell," he said, "from one who lived in Madame's time and used to make the ointments for her or get them made, Stephen Mathé was his name, a canon of the Palace, who before he entered the Church had been surgeon to King Louis XI, the father of the holy lady : he liked well that the noble princess should apply the said ointments with her own hands, for thereby they seemed to have the greater virtue and effect . . . and the said Sir Stephen Mathé lives yet, and can bear testimony to this."

The same witness continued: "The holy lady was so filled with mercy and compassion towards the poor that with her own hands she would dress the ulcers the poor women had upon their legs, going down upon her knees before them so as to dress them with the greater ease, and anointing their wounds so gently and kindly as to be a model of charity and compassion to all that beheld her. And by her very touch," he added, "the said wounds were healed."

The year of Joan's coming to Bourges, 1499, saw the outbreak of a terrible epidemic. Many families fled from the infection, and the Duchess was urged to follow their example and leave the city. She refused to go. The people, she said, were her responsibility. Throughout those anxious months she remained in Bourges. Public prayers were offered to implore the mercy of Heaven. The civic authorities had a model of the city made in wax, with all its walls and towers, weighing 466 pounds; they carried it to the Cathedral and offered it up in a special service of intercession, that the pestilence might be stayed. It abated for a time, but returned the following year: again Joan devoted herself, body and soul, to the needs of her subjects.

So true and tender a charity towards the poor could come only from a heart which was aflame with the love of God. The pitiful compassion for the Wounds of Christ, which she had known from early childhood, became now the grand passion of her life. In her garden she had a Calvary erected, and here she would spend many hours, meditating with love and tears upon the sufferings of Christ upon the Cross. The old gardener who witnessed her devotions was bribed, by dishes sent from her own table, to keep out visitors.

She herself ate meagrely and simply, fasting two days a week, mortifying herself at all times. The splendid dresses of velvet and silk in which she entertained her guests often concealed a haircloth and an iron chain which chafed her skin. It was at this time, too, that she contrived the strange implement of penance made out of her broken lute. She would rise at night, after her waiting-women had left her, and give herself the discipline. The vision of Christ suffering was continually before her eyes and she could not endure that hers should be a life of ease and comfort.

The desire to increase the knowledge of God in the minds of men led her to become an ardent supporter of schemes of education. The University of Bourges was in a bad state. Ignorance and cupidity had taken the place of learning and scholarship, and degrees were being bought and sold for money. She came across an honest man, one Francis Rogier, who was attempting to set up a school of his own under the title of St. Mary's College. She encouraged him to persevere in his project, and found the necessary funds: no easy matter, for she had no capital to draw upon, and it was only when a legacy came to her from a distant source, the house of Armagnac, that she was assured of sufficient money to cover the cost of endowment.

Her interest in this college never flagged, and we find her making provision for it in her will. She leaves money for the free education of ten poor scholars, and expresses her wishes as to their mode of life.

"In the first place, as to their dress, seeing that it is my disposition and intention that they shall always be poor boys who would otherwise be unable to engage in study, and moreover that they shall be desirous of entering religion in one of the Orders approved by our holy Mother the Church, whichever they like best, I will and ordain that they shall wear a habit similar to that of the lay brothers of my Order hereinafter described, of which I am the foundress, and that they shall say the Hours as ordained for the said brothers in their rule, that is to say, the Ave Marias and Pater Nosters; and that every day they shall hear Mass according to the rule of the choir brothers of the said Order: and that the priest engaged to say the said Mass shall be one of the ten, and I will and ordain that he shall always be the Principal of the College, holding a position similar to that of the Principals of the Colleges of Navarre and Montagu at Paris: and I will also that the scholars shall live and eat in common, and when they shall be licensed in theology, they shall be under the obligation, Principal and scholars alike, of setting in their places others, that these also may study and profit until such time as they may acquire the said degree or licence."

For the unlettered, too, she found a way of instruction and edification. In June 1499 there was produced in Bourges, with her encouragement, a great pageant of the Passion of Our Lord, all the parts being played by the clergy, the University students and the young scholars. It was a spectacle calculated to enkindle the hearts of the poorest and least instructed of her subjects.

Churches and religious houses all found in the Duchess a friend and benefactress; but to the Convent of St. Laurence she was something more.

This was a convent of Benedictine nuns. As was the case with many of the religious houses of the time, the primitive rule had been mitigated and discipline had become relaxed. The nuns were accustomed to receive visits and to return them, to enter freely into the social life of the city.

Joan found this state of things unsatisfactory. It did not seem to her to be the right kind of life for women who had renounced the world in order to serve God.

She took counsel with the Archbishop of Bourges and the Abbot of St. Sulpice, her very good friends. Was there any possibility of reforming these nuns? They bade her go ahead and see what she could do.

She paid several friendly visits; dropped a few gentle hints that all was not as it should be. No notice was taken. Then one day she spoke directly and to the point. "This is not right," she said. "We must restore the enclosure."

There was an outcry on the part of the Abbess. The nuns, she declared, were keeping their rule. They had entered Religion, taken it as they found it, and she did not see the necessity for any alteration. In any case, she said, it would be most unfair that those who had entered under one rule should be compelled to accept another and stricter one.

The community supported their Superior. Some of them had much to say on the matter, and not in the most respectful terms. The Duchess was quite unmoved. "Enclosure is indispensable," she said, "and I need your help to enforce it."

The following morning she sent in workmen to close up the doors of the convent. It was the signal for a battle royal. As fast as the men succeeded in securing one door, the nuns, demented with anger, would run round and break down another. The air was filled with cries and shouts of abuse.

Joan did not give up heart: neither did she employ any weapons other than firmness, gentleness, and charity. She pleaded with them, begged them to think of the chances they were throwing away, of the priceless gift of their religious vocation, of the need of the world for prayer and penance. Little by little she prevailed. They calmed down, listened to her burning exhortations. The battle was won.

Six nuns, lent for a time from the Abbey of Notre Dame de Charenton, completed the reformation. The Convent of St. Laurence became a model of religious fervour.

CHAPTER VIII

THE BEGINNINGS OF THE ANNONCIADE

THE life of Joan of France, advancing steeply up the slope of sanctity, was directed at this time by Gilbert Nicholas. This saintly friar, now venerated as Blessed, was a native of Auvergne, born near Riom, about the year 1461. His parents were people of substance and holiness of life. Gilbert was their third child. Two of his nephews followed him into the Order of St. Francis, and a niece, Frances Guyard, became a nun in the Order of the Annonciade. She is the author of the Chronicle from which we derive so many charming details regarding the early days of the Order and the characters of its two founders, Joan of France and Gilbert Nicholas.

The latter, as a child, was gentle and attractive, intelligent and anxious to learn. St. Catherine was his favourite saint at this time, and as a schoolboy it was his custom to turn to her for help with his studies and put up candles at her altar when he had difficulty in memorising a lesson.

He was still only a boy when he fell in love. "While he was yet in his father's house," the chronicler tells us, "he fixed his affections upon a young girl, so much so that he was never happy except when he beheld her." There was no evil in his love, she hastens to assure us, "but when he was absent from the sight of this girl, he was sad." It so happened that on the feast of the Immaculate Conception he heard a sermon preached on the purity and perfections of our blessed Lady. The result was a complete transformation. Never again, he felt, could he desire any woman other than the fair and stainless one, "his Lady, his Mother, and his Friend."

He was of delicate health. Being resolved to enter Religion, and not daring to tell his parents, he stole away secretly, and presented himself at the Franciscan Friary at Meung-sur-Loire. They looked at him, and refused to accept him. He was far too frail, they said, for the life of a friar. He went on to Amboise, and had no better success. The friars of that convent also rejected him, "for which," the Chronicle tells us, "they have since greatly repented."

Sorrowfully he turned away and directed his steps to La Rochelle for a third attempt. He begged admittance, telling truthfully and honestly the story of his previous failures. The friars considered him carefully. He might be delicate, they thought, but "since he had been refused in other places, and had still nowise lost his devotion but rather persevered therein, he might, in time to come, bring forth fruit in the religious life." Accordingly they accepted him and gave him the habit, "which he received in great devotion and reverence, having no regret for the leaving of father and mother, or the goods and pleasures of the world."

He was a very zealous novice, always trying to do more than his share of the work, and constantly seeking to be the last to leave the church. For this, we are told, his superior checked him, teaching him a lesson in obedience he never forgot.

Ordained priest, he commenced his evangelic work, preaching, confessing, drawing souls to God. Profound in learning, he made little of it, and never sought honours in the world of the Schools. He did an immense amount of work for Joan of France, and undertook many travels and fatigues on behalf of her Order; yet with this he combined the duties successively of Father Guardian at Amboise, Provincial of Aquitaine, and three times Commissary-General of his Order "beyond the Alps," that is to say, of all Europe with the exception of Italy.

It was in 1518, thirteen years after the death of Joan, that Pope Leo X, in token of his veneration for Gilbert Nicholas, gave him the name of Gabriel-Maria, the name by which he is best known, and by which it will be convenient to call him henceforth. It is told that on this occasion, as he was taking leave of the Pope, he knelt to kiss his feet, and the Pope, bending down, kissed him gently on the tonsure.

Gabriel-Maria and his saintly penitent first met at Amboise, at a time when the ageing Jean de la Fontaine bequeathed to him the holy soul whom he himself had directed ever since she was a little child of five. Precisely when this meeting occurred is uncertain. The part of the chronicle which describes Joan's life previous to her coming to Bourges is short and inaccurate, which looks as though Fr. Gabriel-Maria, from whom the chronicler derived much of her information, was not well acquainted with this part of her life. He is first mentioned immediately after the Nullity Process, and from then onwards until her death Joan was always in touch with him, though at times, when his duties took him elsewhere, he would delegate his charge to one of his brethren.

He was a gentle director, but extremely strict. Discouragements and failings due to human nature always evoked his sympathy and understanding; sin and scandal he dealt with severely. Bishop Dony d'Attichy, one of his earliest biographers, likened him to a bee, "which with its honey hath also its sting." Above all, he was a man of prayer. The sound of the bell, the striking of the clock, to him was the reminder to say *Ave Maria*. "There was never a single moment that he had not the praises of God or of His holy Mother, either in his heart or on his tongue, whether going or coming, eating or drinking, waking or sleeping."

It was to Gabriel-Maria then, very soon after her arrival in Bourges, that the Duchess of Berry opened her heart.

"Father," she said, "I must reveal to you the desire which God has given me this long time past, to found an Order of the glorious Virgin Mary, an Order of Religious who shall be ruled by you and the friars of the Order of St. Francis of the Observance."

"Madame," the good friar answered, "I revere your holy desire, for it is good and holy, and proceeds, I think, from the Holy Spirit. But it is always difficult to introduce a new Order into the Church. You would certainly find great difficulty and opposition. It would be far better, if you have the desire of founding a convent of nuns to pray for you and yours, to found one of St. Clare, like the Convent of Ave Maria of the Poor Clares at Paris: they are governed by the Friars of the Observance."

She was disappointed, but made no comment except to say: "Father, if it is the will of God and his blessed Mother, they will help me in this affair;" and there the matter was allowed to drop.

So the first year passed. Gabriel-Maria was away at Amboise and Joan was busy with the affairs of her duchy. It was the time when the pestilence was raging, and she was worn out with work by day and prayer by night. When Gabriel-Maria returned in the March of 1500, he found her far from well.

"When she saw him," the chronicle tells us, "and they two were alone together, she said to him: 'Father, you are the cause of my illness, maybe of my death!' He showed himself, as we may well believe, right sorrowful and concerned at such a word. Then the holy Lady said to him: 'Since you are so grieved of my distress, oh, will you not aid me to accomplish my desire of raising up an Order of Religion of the Virgin Mary?' "

So she reproached him gently, full of trust in his will to guide and comfort her.

" 'I am constrained,' she went on, 'by God and his blessed Mother to reveal to you the secret of my heart. But before I speak it, promise me that you will do all that I ask, that shall be to the honour of the Virgin Mary.' "

He promised, and she continued:

" 'Father, by the grace of God, and not by merit

of mine, when I was yet a little girl, being one day at Mass before the image of the Virgin Mary and the Crucifix, a thought came striking at my heart, and said to me, 'Before thy death, thou shalt found an order of the Virgin Mary, and in so doing, thou shalt give great pleasure and honour to me, the blessed mother of God.' And ever since that hour my desire has increased, and I promised the Virgin Mary that when I should be at liberty, I would bring the desire to accomplishment. Therefore, Father, I beg of you, delay no longer to heed me, but help and counsel me all you know, what I am to do; for I would wish to spare nothing in this matter, neither myself nor all my possessions.' "

Father Gabriel-Maria answered her, "Madame, if you had been pleased to tell me your secret before this, I would not have delayed to help you." He went on to remind her that such a project could not be undertaken without much prayer and consideration, but since it seemed to be divinely inspired he would do everything in his power to help her. She was overjoyed, and her health began rapidly to improve.

Some days later, after they had both prayed fervently for light, Father Gabriel-Maria reiterated that it would be no easy thing to found a new order in the Church, but that with the help of our Lord and his holy Mother it could be done. He bade her take note that the old orders all differed from one another, that of St. Benedict being distinct from those of St. Francis and St. Bernard, and so on: the new order would be something entirely different from anything that had gone before. "The Order of the

Virgin Mary will have no other patron, no kind of life, no pattern other than that of the Virgin Mary alone. And that is only right, for she is Lady and Queen of Angels and Saints: and all that she did in this world she did not from human example, but by the Holy Ghost her Teacher, who directed all her thoughts, words and holy works to the honour of God and the edification of souls. Wherefore, in your Order, pay no heed to other forms, but contemplate all that the Lady of Virtues did, and take from her the life which your nuns are to lead."

He then went on to the practical side of the matter. "Get a house," he said, "near the palace, with two or three rooms furnished with beds and other necessaries. There you can house the girls with whom you are to found your Order, and there they can learn the proper rites and ceremonies. I will give you two friars, Girard Pasquet and Ambrose Basset, to train them in the religious life, so that by the time the convent is built they will be all ready and able to enter the enclosure."

Where were they to find the right sort of girls? the Duchess wanted to know: " they must be of substantial and honourable families, of good repute and character, and they must have a genuine desire to persevere for life in a reformed Order. They must not be artful or flighty."

He reassured her. At Tours, he told her, there was living a certain lady with whom he was acquainted. She kept a school in which were educated the daughters of all the chief people in the town. She was very devout, and her house was conducted almost like a convent. With her help they would be sure to find some postulants of the right type.

Lent came, and Father Gabriel-Maria was due back at his convent in Amboise. As soon as he arrived there, his first care was to send a message to Dame Macée la Pourcelle at Tours, begging her to have the kindness to come over and see him, as he had a secret commission to entrust to her on behalf of the Duchess of Berry. She came, and he laid the matter before her.

"Father," she answered, "I think I have in my house just the very girls that you and Madame are wanting, and I know others of good family in Tours. But I rather fear that their parents will be unwilling to let them go so far away."

"Let their parents know," he told her : "do everything you possibly can to please Madame."

"Father," she said, "please tell Madame that I am her humble servant, very ready to perform her commission. I shall set to work with all possible diligence to find the kind of girls she wants, and those who are still at school I shall try to bring on in the preparation and desire for the religious life. I should deem myself very happy if my pupils were to be found suitable to be the beginning of so great a work as the Order of the Blessed Virgin Mary, and if at some future day I might see them giving honour and service to the holy Mother of God, happy indeed if I might see it accomplished in my lifetime."

Dame la Pourcelle returned to Tours and set to work.

"On the Thursday before the Ascension of our

Lord in the year 1500," the chronicle says, "the venerable Father Guardian of Amboise arrived at the said town of Tours, to the great joy and honour of the house of the good Dame la Pourcelle, at the hour of midday, and he was very welcome to the chief people in the said town, for he was known and well loved. And many great personages, fathers and mothers and brothers of the girls who were scholars with the good Dame, came to see him: and there was ready for him a repast to which each had sent something, for at that time there was great scarcity in the town, and bread especially was very dear."

It was always Father Gabriel-Maria's way, when he was entertained to a meal, to mingle together spiritual and temporal fare. He would put forward a few questions on some spiritual topic, receive the answers, and then give a little talk on the conclusions to be drawn. He did so on this occasion; then, as he continued his meal, he took careful notice of the girls whom the Dame had collected. He asked their names. The first, he was told, was Andrée Jacquelle. She was a boarder and her home was at Amboise. Her parents had come to Tours especially to see the good father. He was delighted. *Andrew*, he said, was the name of the first disciple of our Lord; *Andrée* should be the first to be called by his blessed Mother.

In the evening the father and the good lady had a conference. She had found plenty of suitable girls, she told him; but their parents were making difficulties. They were afraid of the distance and the hardships, afraid their children might meet with treatment other than that to which they had been accustomed. He bade her tell them they need have no fear. Their daughters would be well looked after and would lack nothing.

The following morning Father Gabriel-Maria interviewed the girls again, eleven in all. Their names were Andrée Jacquelle, Marguerite and Marie Bodine, Jeanne Jovere, Marguerite Blandine, Marie Garelle, Perrine Fouchere, Denise Durande, Jeanne Chevalier, Jeanne Brett and Antoinette Phelippon, all, with the exception of the first, natives of Tours. Gabriel-Maria was very pleased with them. He made them a little discourse, bidding them be of good heart and courage, to have a great desire to serve God and the glorious Virgin Mary, and not to be afraid of leaving their parents and homes, but to follow the example of Abraham, who left everything to obey God. So would they come to the Promised Land of Heaven. He had them in one by one to talk to him. All desired "to leave the world, and their parents and friends, in order to be spouses of Jesus and religious of the Virgin Mary, and daughters of the holy Duchess of Berry."

Gabriel-Maria was very happy. He made arrangements with the good Dame to bring them herself to Bourges; he gave them his blessing, and went on ahead to prepare the Duchess for their coming.

The party left Tours the following day. Father Gabriel-Maria had counselled them to begin their journey on the Saturday, our Lady's day, but to travel only a short stage. Accordingly they set out after Vespers.

They were accommodated in two *charettes*, long,

wheeled wagons, the eleven of them with their boxes and all their belongings, the Dame, and a guide whom the Duchess had appointed to make the arrangements and pay the charges. Poor Dame la Pourcelle had had an anxious time persuading parents not to back out at the eleventh hour but to let their daughters go. The mother of the two Bodine girls made her promise most faithfully that she would bring them back with her. Since they had given in their names, their mother said, they might go and see *Madame la duchesse*, but they were not on any account to remain. The mother and brother of Andrée Jacquelle and the relatives of some of the other girls accompanied the party.

It was May, loveliest season of the year. As they drove out and turned to look back upon the walls and roofs of Tours, it must have seemed a fair city to be leaving behind for always; but the children—and children they were, some of them as young as eleven, ten, and even *nine* years of age—winked back their tears, and went on bravely. They halted for the night some five miles out of Tours. On the Sunday morning they heard Mass and then took to the road again.

Their way lay up the Cher, the river running clear and sparkling through a country of rolling hills and green pastures. They were orderly, well-behaved girls, neither "artful nor flighty," as Madame had stipulated; but it is impossible to imagine that they travelled in silence: more likely a continual babble of "Madame la duchesse at Bourges . . .the Order of Madame la duchesse and the Virgin Mary . . . . Madame la duchesse . . ." as the great wagons rolled and creaked along the rutty roads.

Suddenly there was a catastrophe. One of the charettes stuck fast, lurched and shook. There was a tearing crash, a plunging of horses and a chorus of screams, as the clumsy wagon overturned and lay upon its side. One after another the occupants were extricated; it was the wagon in which the younger ones were travelling. All, by the mercy of God, were unhurt. Only the poor Dame lay groaning in pain with a badly crushed arm.

They helped her along to the nearest inn, got linen and bathed and dressed the injured limb. The elder ones busied themselves with their mistress. The rest stood apart in a state of consternation. What was to happen now? They could not possibly go on without the Dame. Must they go back? back to the homes they had never expected to see again, to the friends to whom they had bidden farewell? Must they return to Tours without even having seen Madame la duchesse—or the Order of the Virgin Mary? And they had hoped to be such good nuns!

Some of them began to pray, others to sing a hymn to our Lady. The Dame heard them, and with a heroic effort she pulled herself together. "Children," she said, "don't be distressed about my hurt. The devil is trying to hinder our journey, because he knows that it is tending to the great honour of God and his holy Mother, and to the saving of souls. If it had been one of you that had been injured, we could not have gone on. Let the devil do his worst: he shall not stop us!"

So they went on, the good lady in great pain; and

on Wednesday, the eve of the Ascension, at ten o'clock in the morning, they entered the city of Bourges, and were deposited at an inn near the monastery of St. Sulpice.

The Duchess, notified of their arrival, sent for them to come to her at eight o'clock that same evening. Her reason for selecting so late an hour was her desire for secrecy. Up to the present her plans were known to very few people. At the appointed hour the Dame and her pupils, rested and refreshed, were admitted at a side door by Marie Pot. It was getting dark. She lit torches, and conducted them along passages to the hall where Joan was awaiting them. Only Marie and Mme. d'Aumont were in attendance.

The girls entered and dropped their best curtseys. Then Dame la Pourcelle stepped forward.

"Madame," she said, "these are the girls whom I was commissioned, by the venerable Father Guardian of the Convent at Amboise, to find and bring to you, a service which I have been very happy to perform. They are all girls of good will, good character, good repute and family, children of wealthy and honourable parents. I present them to you, trusting you will find them to your liking."

Joan looked at them, and her heart warmed to these children. They were all so young, so earnest, so unspoilt. Perhaps in that hour when she first heard their names, the thought may have crossed her mind that, had things been different in her life, it might have been her own little Jeanne or Marie that she was training up to offer to the Mother of God. "He who maketh the barren woman to dwell in the house, the happy mother of children," may well have been her prayer of thanksgiving that night. Henceforth they were to be her *children*, her *daughters*, the first of all the charges upon her love, her energies and her prayers.

She thanked the Dame warmly for the trouble she had taken, then she had a word with each girl in turn, wishing to discover their aptitudes and capabilities. How much had they learnt, she asked them, and what did they know about keeping house? And again she expressed her approval and thanks to the Dame.

Where was Father Gabriel-Maria? No one knew. Dame la Pourcelle could only say that he had gone on ahead and promised to meet them at Bourges. The Duchess sent off to Amboise the following morning to discover what had become of him. He was found to be very ill with pleurisy. It was three weeks before he was able to join them in Bourges. The Duchess sent her own physician and apothecary to look after him. So did the King!

Meanwhile the new postulants were taken to the house that had been got ready for them. Mme. d'Aumont conducted them and delivered them into the keeping of a pious old lady, Mme. d'Aurouës, who, with her servant Catherine Ragonne, was henceforth to have charge of them. It was a two-storied house, and the upstairs room had been furnished with rope beds covered with feather mattresses. The girls felt them doubtfully, thinking of the comfortable curtained beds they had left at home. The sheets were coarse, "like sackcloth," one whispered to another. It all seemed very strange. Possibly there was more than one fit of the giggles before they all settled down for the night; probably some of their rough pillows were wet with tears. Who will blame them? They were not nuns yet. They were only a parcel of schoolgirls, on the brink of a tremendous adventure.

CHAPTER IX

THE ORDER OF THE BLESSED VIRGIN MARY

THIS being the story of Joan of France, we must not allow ourselves to be drawn away from her by Frances Guyard's very fascinating account of all that happened to the little postulants from Tours. The morning after their arrival in Bourges, being Ascension Day, they heard Mass in the church of Montermoyen, close to their new home. When they returned to the house, the Duchess came in to see them. She had not noticed, on the previous evening, the hurt which Dame la Pourcelle had sustained on the journey; it says much for her absorption in her new daughters that she had been so unobservant. When she did discover it, her concern was great, and she hastened to afford the good lady every possible attention.

At length Father Gabriel-Maria arrived, having recovered from his illness, and was made very welcome. His coming was a joy and stimulus to them all. He put new heart into the postulants by describing to them all the happiness they might look for in the religious life. He calmed the fears of their relatives by assuring them of the love and care with which Madame would watch over their daughters. Dame la Pourcelle then prepared to depart. She had grave misgivings about leaving the two Bodines behind, after the promise she had made to their mother, but both girls declared that "they would rather die than return, and they willed to be religious of the Order of the Virgin Mary." The Duchess took them lovingly in her arms. It would never do, she said, for God and his blessed Mother to be robbed of these two, who were offering themselves with so good a heart. Father Gabriel-Maria agreed with her. If there were any sin in breaking the promise, they said, he and she would take it upon their own consciences. Accordingly Dame la Pourcelle "took kindly leave of all her girls, not without tears on either side: and she admonished them and prayed them to be good girls, devout, gentle, and tractable, doing credit by their good conversation to their parents and friends, and to herself who had been their teacher: and she prayed them to be sensible of the favour that our Lord and the Virgin Mary were showing them in calling them to be the first in so holy an estate as the commencement of the order of the Virgin Mary. She commended herself right heartily to their prayers, and left them in the care of our Lord and his blessed Mother, to whom she entrusted them, and gave them her blessing. Which done, she returned to Tours with the good Dame Jacquelle and the other parents who had come to accompany the said girls."

When she had gone, Gabriel-Maria and the Duchess took careful stock of their postulants. Some of them could read well, some had a slight knowledge of letters, others none at all. Reading, at that time, was a rare accomplishment. It was one, all the same, which Joan's daughters were to have. It was her wish that they should learn to recite the Divine Office. Marguerite Blandine was the best scholar among them, and to her was assigned the task of teaching the others. They were to begin straight away to learn the psalms. Father Gabriel-Maria, consulted, suggested that they should recite ten psalms every day, five after Matins, five after Compline. They might use the Office of the Blessed Virgin Mary until such time as they could attempt the Office of the Roman breviary.

The daily régime was laid down. Between four and five in the morning they rose and said Matins, followed by the five psalms, then Prime and Terce. After that they would go in silence to the Church of Montermoyen to hear Mass : on their return, Sext, followed by reading, private devotions or household tasks till dinner-time. After dinner, recreation in the garden until midday, then an hour's prayer or reading. At one o'clock None: after that such tasks as might be given them, "for above all things they must not be idle or waste their time." At three o'clock Vespers were said, and supper followed at four: after grace, recreation until Compline and the five psalms at six, then night-prayers, and at seven o'clock bed, in complete silence. It was not an easy rule, and Madame and the good Father saw to it that it was strictly kept; for, they said, "if they were negligent in punishing and correcting small faults, they would fall from trivial into greater ones."

Friar Girard was made responsible for training them in the liturgy. He taught them how to say the

Office, how to stand, to bow, to alternate the versicles. He was very particular. He never passed over the slightest mistake. Friar Ambrose was appointed to assist him, and to be their confessor. Confession once a fortnight was the rule, and Holy Communion on all the great feasts of our Lord and our Lady.

It was a hard life for such young girls; but they took to it with courage and gladness. Joan in her daily intercourse succeeded in instilling into them much of her own zeal. Not a day passed but she would come in and talk to them, and it was their great joy to listen to her. They loved her dearly, but they feared her, too ; they feared above all things that they might fall short of the standard which she set before them. They accepted, with love and determination, all the hardships which their life entailed, the little ones as much so as their elders; and in truth their life was harder than Joan meant it to be, for, all unknown to her, the old lady who looked after them fed them very badly. "Bread, black as earth," and very little of that, was what she gave them. "And the poor girls took it in patience for the love of our Saviour, that in time to come they might be good religious and not find poverty too grievous." When the Duchess discovered this state of affairs she put an end to it at once. It had been no part of her plan that her children should be starved. After this she took an active part in kitchen affairs, revealing an acquaintance with domestic economy scarcely to be expected in one of her position.

And the beds, those strange beds that had worried them so much the first night: it was not long before, as Frances Guyard tells us, "when they were all alone, thinking that no one would come into their rooms again, they would take away the mattresses and lie devoutly on the ropes, telling one another that they must make a start and do penance, seeing that they had entered religion for that purpose, and that our blessed Saviour had suffered so much for them, bedded so hardly in the crib and on the cross."

So was the work begun. After some months Joan began to feel that it was time to take the next step. Accordingly she sent for Father Gabriel-Maria.

He came very willingly, and went in to see the girls, inquiring eagerly of their doings and progress. Afterwards the Duchess said to him, "Father, let us talk about my Order. The number of my girls is increasing, and they are not really safe where they are. My convent will not be built all in a day. I want your advice. What should I do first?"

Father Gabriel-Maria did not answer her immediately. He began by making a test of her humility. Instead of the kindly counsel she had looked for, she got a stinging rebuke:

"Madame," he said, "I believe you think of nothing else but your girls and your Order, and neglect and forget God and your own conscience, virtues and perfection. Tell me first, what progress have you yourself made in the spiritual exercises I gave you?"

Possibly the check was justified. Even a saint may need to be reminded at times that it is God who gives the increase, and that in the greatest of all prayers, the word "I" does not appear. Joan took it all in good part. "The holy lady," the chronicle says, "went down upon her knees before him, accusing herself of so many faults past and present that the good Father raised his eyes to Heaven, praying to our Saviour that he would be pleased to grant him, through the merits of this holy lady, a portion of her humility." Nevertheless he continued sternly: "You who are the root and the trunk of the tree which is your order, who by your imperfections have robbed it of its moisture, so that it dries up and cannot bring forth the fruits of sweetness and good odour before God and his holy Mother—how think you that your daughters will profit, if you yourself be not the first in virtue?"

Then the chronicler goes on to reveal the secret which lay behind these hard words. There was an agreement between these two, a promise made to our Lady, that either might say to the other, or ask of the other, anything whatsoever, without fear of resentment or refusal. It was a mutual promise. It speaks volumes for the confidence which Gabriel-Maria inspired in his penitent, and she in him. It comes as a sudden revelation of depths of sanctity hitherto unsuspected.

The good father had a shrewd suspicion that Joan had something special to tell him. He was convinced that God would never have inspired her to found an order without giving her also some indication as to its nature and rule. Having, as it were, recalled to her mind the pact which lay between them, he went on to question her:

"Madame and daughter," he said, "you told me of the revelation you received in your youth to raise up an order of the Virgin Mary. Now tell me, have you not had some revelation or inspiration also as to how the rule should be composed, and on what perfections, whether of Jesus or his Mother, it should be based?"

It was the question she dreaded, for she feared by her very answer to offend against the humility which he so strove to cultivate in her; but answer she must.

> "Father," she said, "you know the desire that I have always had from my youth, to give pleasure to the blessed Virgin Mary. Well, one day I was greatly desirous to discover in what way I could please her most, and I prayed with all my heart during Mass that she would let me know what manner of life I was to lead, and those of my order with me, so as to accomplish her good pleasure in all things, and the pleasure of Jesus her Son: and then—I seemed to be lifted right out of myself, carried half away: and I was aware that I was in the presence of the holy Mother and my God, and I begged her with all my heart for the fulfilment of my desire. Then she answered me : 'Write down everything I did in the world which is told in the Gospels. Make a rule from that, and get it approved by the Holy See. And know this, that you and all those, men and women, who shall be willing to abide by this rule, shall be in the grace of God my Son and me, and shall find in it a sure way to accomplish the good pleasure of us both.' "

It was agreed that Father Gabriel-Maria should

draw up the rule according to these instructions, Joan and her daughters praying earnestly for his guidance. He did so. He drew up a rule under ten headings, each dealing with a particular virtue exhibited by Mary in the holy Gospels. He could, he explained, have thought of others: but, faithful to the revelation granted to Joan, he confined himself to those which the Evangelists record. When the rule was completed he presented it to Madame, who found it "good, holy and to her pleasure." A certain friar, William Morin by name, was chosen to convey the rule to Rome for the Apostolic approbation.

Friar William duly arrived in Rome, and presented his petition to Pope Alexander VI, who examined it and declared himself favourably impressed. The College of Cardinals, however, was less favourable; there was a strong feeling against any innovation in the way of religious orders. Their decision was a definite refusal. The poor father came away disconsolate, and to add to his troubles he had the misfortune on the way to lose the precious rule, and had to return unsuccessful and empty-handed. It was a terrible blow, but it fell upon hearts accustomed to deal with tribulation. To quote the chronicle again: "Father Gabriel-Maria, seeing that Madame was very sad, spoke to her as saint Gabriel spoke to Mary when he announced that she would be the Mother of God. 'Madame, be not troubled or sad,' he said : 'sweet Jesus and his holy Mother permit that you meet with this hindrance to your desire to do them honour so that in the end you may receive the greater merit. I said to you that matters such as these are not accomplished all at once. So does God reveal to you the love he bears you. What if the holy Father has refused to approve your rule? God and his Mother are greater than he, they will see to it. Put your trust in them. What if the rule has been lost? Remember that it was the same with our father St. Francis. The Virgin Mary surely knew that there were faults in the rule, faults of which you and I knew nothing: that is why she has permitted it to be lost. Turn to her, pray that she may give me of her spirit, and in her honour I will write another. Then, if it please you, I shall go myself to Rome to present it to our Holy Father, for it may be that the Virgin Mary is not well pleased that for her sake I would not take so much trouble myself the first time.' "

So it was done. The new rule was written and approved, and Father Gabriel-Maria set off for Rome, leaving behind him earnest and anxious hearts. "For in those days," Frances Guyard tells us, writing from the advanced standpoint of the year 1561, "the road to Rome was not taken as commonly as it is at the present, by reason that it was much more dangerous. So Madame gave him a troop of men for an escort. And he, before he departed, went to take leave of the young girls from Tours, and their converse was not without tears for the length of the road which lay before him, and the fear that hurt or ill fortune might befall him. He commended himself heartily to their prayers. And oftentimes Madame would come and talk of him during his journey."

While Father Gabriel-Maria was absent, Joan applied for another necessary approbation of her design, that of the King. This was readily afforded. The document granting the formal Royal permission is dated March 1504.

The good father duly arrived in Rome, after some adventures on the way. So at least we infer from the chronicler, for she tells us that, as he returned, "he beheld here and there the bones of some of those who had been his escort as he came." Gabriel-Maria submitted the rule anew, and made his petition. He fared no better than his predecessor. The cardinals held fast to the decision of the fourth Lateran Council, that religious orders should not be multiplied: better to reform and improve the many already in existence. The Pope could only acquiesce. Let Madame, he said, found a convent of any order she chose. She should have every facility, every privilege, every indulgence he could grant her: but a new order—no, it was out of the question.

Gabriel-Maria did not despair. He knew that, on earth, the Holy Father was supreme; but "God and his Blessed Mother are greater than he." So he had told Joan. He went on praying. "He prayed to God till evening came, and all the night that followed he went on with fervent prayers and supplications to God and his holy Mother."

Morning came, and he said his Mass. Afterwards, as he was descending the stairs, a messenger met him in haste, coming from Cardinal Ferraro, Chancellor of the Datary. This was the prelate who had been most emphatic in opposing the project. Now he was all eager to help. During the past night the Cardinal had seen in a vision St. Francis and St. Laurence:

they bade him, "Accomplish the work which the father is doing for this Duchess and Lady." After that, all went smoothly. The Pope and cardinals, seeing the conversion of the Chancellor, withdrew their objections. The rule, when examined, was found to contain nothing that was new, for it was based entirely upon scriptural texts. Such innovation as there was lay, not in the end for which the order was to be instituted, but rather in the means to be employed. Other orders had been founded under Mary's patronage whose object was the contemplation of God. Others again, engaging in active good works, had taken her for their model; but it was left to Joan of France and Gabriel-Maria, under divine inspiration, to initiate an order which had for its sole end the praise and glory of God, and for its sole means the imitation, the *reproduction* of Mary. The religious of the order of the Blessed Virgin Mary were to be so many living copies of Mary, imitating her virtues, thinking her thoughts, living her life. Mary, Queen of Angels and men, our constant intercessor in the sight of God, is yet a creature who, during her life on earth, by faithful co-operation with God's grace became his masterpiece, most perfect work of his hands. No human being has ever come nearer to him than she, none has ever succeeded in giving him better service. If we would seek to do him pleasure, we cannot improve upon Mary's methods. The design, therefore, which Joan and her holy director had in mind, was that they, and others after them, should model themselves as closely as possible upon our Blessed Lady, *impersonate* her as it were, in so far as sinners may impersonate the Sinless. The Rule of the Order was made up of a kind of picture of Mary as she was in her earthly life, a picture which other human beings might strive to reproduce. It was based upon all the texts in the Gospels in which Mary's lovely nature is revealed.

Mary knew no law except the Will of God, no guide other than the charity of God. For her it sufficed. "If you love me," Christ said, "keep my commandments." Her sanctity grew naturally out of God's love for her and hers for him.

The method adopted by Father Gabriel-Maria was to go through the Gospel texts and draw from each one particular aspect of the fullness of grace with which Mary was endowed. In all he found ten. To these ten manifestations of her sanctity he gave the name of the Ten Virtues or Ten Perfections of Mary. These, arranged in order as they appear in the Gospel—an order that was slightly changed later, as one virtue seemed to demand precedence over the others—were: Prudence, Purity, Humility, Faith, Prayerfulness, Obedience, Poverty, Patience, Charity and Compassion.

The virtue of *Prudence* he found in the words: "Mary was troubled at his saying, and thought with herself what manner of salutation this should be": and again, "His Mother kept all these words in her heart."

Mary was slow to speak. Her words, when they came, were humble, gentle and to the point, but they were never spoken without reflection. She listened to God speaking in her heart, guiding, warning, enlightening. Her daughters, imitating her, learn to "watch and pray," to be careful in speech, wise in decision, steadfast in resolution.

The second virtue, in the definitive Rule placed first, is *Purity*. It is exemplified in Mary's words: "How shall this be done, because I know not man?"

Mary's purity was absolute, for she was immaculate, preserved, from the first moment of existence in the womb of her mother, from original sin, and protected by the grace of God from actual sin. Here was the perfect chastity. Her virginity, the oblation of herself to God, was total and unreserved.

Religious, following Mary's example, take a vow of chastity, offering themselves body and soul to Christ, as to their Divine Spouse. In fidelity to him they forgo all other attachments, and eschew all circumstances in life which might lead them to be neglectful of him. Mary is their model and exemplar in this. She in her youth had vowed herself to God, and not even the words of an Angel could move her to be unfaithful to the offering she had made. Only when the Angel assured her that God willed her to be virgin and mother both, did she speak the word giving her consent.

Humility is the third of the Ten Virtues. Gabriel-Maria found it in Mary's words: "Behold the handmaid of the Lord; be it done to me according to thy word."

Mary placed herself utterly at God's disposal. She was his "handmaid," his "slave." (The word in the original Greek means "one born in slavery, having no human rights.") Hers is the purely, selfless attitude. *She* had accomplished nothing. All the goodness was of God. She was his humble creature, claiming nothing as her own except the will to please him, the will which itself was his gift to her. Her sweet virtue of humility was the weapon opposed to Satan's sin of pride. "I will not serve," cried Lucifer, and fell to the depths of Hell; "Lord, behold thy servant," said Mary, and was raised to the heights of Heaven.

The humility of the Blessed Virgin was held up for admiration and imitation to her nuns. The title given to the Superioress was—and remains—"Ancelle," i.e. Ancilla, handmaid, and the Sisters respected and obeyed her as they would the Blessed Virgin herself. Flattery was a thing to be shunned, reproof to be accepted without self-excuse.

The fourth virtue, which we call *Faith*, in the sense of fidelity or loyalty, in the original rule was named *Veritas*, Truth. To the faithful, the truth is revealed. "Blessed art thou," cried Elizabeth to Mary, "that hast believed, because those things shall be accomplished which were spoken to thee by the Lord."

Faith is an act, not of the emotions, but of the intellect and the will. To the one who genuinely seeks to know him and confidently strives to come to him, God grants the vision of the truth. Mary's simple fidelity is an example to her children. They accept with love and submission all the truths which the Catholic Church teaches, avoiding scrupulosity and subtlety of doctrine. The faithful soul holds itself alert, ready to receive the enlightenment of the Spirit and to act promptly and courageously upon his inspirations.

The fifth virtue was *Prayerfulness*, the spirit of worship (in Latin, *Laudabilitas*). "My soul doth magnify the Lord," said Mary, "and my spirit hath rejoiced in God my Saviour."

Our Lady's prayer of praise was a hymn of joy. Her utter selflessness gave all to God, and left no room for repining, or fear, or sense of her own insufficiency. Prayer to her was the spontaneous outpouring of an immaculate heart. In God she found perfect Goodness, Beauty, Truth. She loved him, trusted him, cast herself upon his perfections with all the happiness and abandon of a child.

The spirit of prayer is the characteristic virtue of the contemplative. It is a thing which the world does not understand. To many people prayer appears to be an emotional outlet, a selfish activity which concerns the individual alone. In reality it is something vastly different. It is a tightening of the bonds which knit the soul to God, a sharing, in ever deepening intensity, in the divine nature itself. The saint who prays becomes more and more God-like, sharing in God's attributes, exercising his powers. "I live now, not I," cried St. Paul, "but Christ liveth in me." Something of the omnipotence of God is granted, even in this life, to the man of prayer.

God, in his divine scheme, wills that his gifts should be *asked for*. Christ is "always living to make intercession for us;" Mary his Mother, her heart in perfect unison with his, takes part in his intercession. Even we, the creatures of God, are invited to "ask, that we may receive."

Prayer, then, is the portion, the task, the privilege

of the generous soul which surrenders itself wholly to God. Prayer is the livelihood of such, homage, praise, thanksgiving, intercession, the prayer of the liturgy, the Mass, the Divine Office: personal prayer, vocal and mental. Mary's life was one perpetual prayer. Those who would imitate her must strive to acquire the same spirit, for it is by prayer that souls are brought to accept the fruits of Redemption which Jesus Christ won for them on Calvary.

The sixth of the virtues is *Obedience*. "In those days," says St. Luke, "there went forth a decree from Caesar Augustus."

The virtue of Obedience consists in the oblation of one's own will to God, subjecting it to the decree of a lawful superior. Joseph and Mary were subjects of Caesar Augustus. When his edict was proclaimed they obeyed, simply, humbly, and without question. Their obedience entailed much hardship and danger; in view of the great event which was impending, it might have been considered unreasonable and unnecessary, but that was not the view they took of it. Caesar was their lawful ruler, entrusted with power from God. In that sense, he occupied God's place: therefore they obeyed him.

In a religious house every act, no matter how trivial, is regulated by obedience to the Rule and to the Superior. Actions performed in this spirit acquire a double merit, for to the act itself is added the sacrifice of self which obedience requires.

The seventh virtue is *Poverty*, the practice of the oblation of one's possessions and of the right to possess. It follows naturally upon the sixth, for if by obedience we *give* all to God, by poverty we learn to *accept* everything as coming from his hands.

Mary was well acquainted with poverty. The night she brought her Son into the world she had very little of the world's goods to offer him. "She wrapped him up in swaddling-clothes, and laid him in a manger." God might, had he so willed it, have arranged that his Son should be born in a palace, surrounded by comfort and luxury; instead, he chose the shelter of a cold bare cave. His Mother was prepared to accept the one or the other with equal willingness. She had no desire to possess anything except what God willed her to have. Following her example, her daughters choose to reject luxury and superfluity. By so doing they come to realise the Providence of God and his loving care for all their needs.

The eighth of Mary's virtues is *Patience*, the acceptance of hardship. This beautiful combination of fortitude and trust sustained her throughout all the trials of her life. "Fly into Egypt:" "Son, why hast thou done so to us? Behold thy father and I have sought thee sorrowing." There was no sense of rebellion in Mary's words. Her fortitude waxed as her troubles increased, and her confidence in God never failed.

Charity (*pietas*) is the ninth virtue, seen in Mary's solicitude for the kindly couple who were giving her hospitality. "Son," she said in gentle tones, "they have no wine;" and so great was the love in which he held her that he could not resist her appeal.

Followers of Mary must above all things have

charity. One of Joan's maxims to her daughters was : "Every night before retiring the Mother Handmaid should *cover the fire*;" meaning that no disagreement or grievance should be allowed to persist into another day. If the Sisters are not in charity with one another, they can not love God and Mary.

Tenth of the virtues is *Compassion.* "There stood by the cross of Jesus, Mary his Mother. . . ." None can ever hope to imitate Our Blessed Lady unless he be prepared to enter into her sufferings, to stand beside her at the foot of the Cross. Joan of France had been accustomed from her childhood to meditate deeply upon the Wounds of Christ. At Bourges she had made the Calvary in her garden her favourite place of resort. In her own life she had known sorrow and humiliation and loss. By sharing these with Mary she had come to know the consolation of strength. By offering to her divine Saviour the gift of her compassionate heart, she set the seal of perfection upon the copy of Mary which she was seeking to reproduce. So it was with her daughters. All the trials and hardships of their life were borne in union with Mary, for the salvation of souls; and in honour of her days of mourning, the Friday and Saturday of every week were observed as days of fasting.

Such was the Rule of the Ten Virtues or Ten Perfections of Mary, the aim of which was to give honour and glory to God by imitating the life of Mary, most perfect of his creatures. On the twelfth of February 1502 the rule was formally approved under the seal of the Holy See. Father Gabriel-Maria returned in triumph. On the journey home he had more misadventures, for while travelling in mountainous country he slipped and fell from a considerable height. He held on tight to the precious rule, and to that circumstance attributed his preservation from injury.

The name given to the order in the Bull of Approbation was "The Order of the Blessed Virgin Mary," and this remains its true and proper title. The convent at Bourges was placed under the patronage of Our Lady of the Annunciation, "l'Annonciade," in old French "La Nonciade." This title of the motherhouse came to be applied to the whole Order, so that it was commonly spoken of as "the Order of the Annonciade."

There was yet a third title, redolent of the romantic poetry of the day: the "Order of the Ten Pleasures or Virtues of Mary": Mary's good pleasure, her will or choice: Mary's Virtues, her ways or methods of perfection. It was an apt title, for it summed up in a phrase the whole purport of the Order: to imitate Mary, to choose her way, in so doing to offer to God the most perfect form of service which a creature could possibly render to him.

To imitate Mary, to reproduce her, to bring her to the souls that need her, and through her to lay their needs before the throne of God's mercy—this is what mankind, consciously or unconsciously, has always craved for. To help supply this need, Joan of France found the means to "serve and give pleasure" to God, by raising up many faithful souls in whom Mary's virtues should be reproduced.

CHAPTER X

THE ANNONCIADE IS ESTABLISHED

THE postulants were preparing, the Rule was approved. The next pressing matter was to get the convent built, for the present house was inconvenient and insecure. Already the girls had had one fright, when a man was found trying to clamber in at an upper window. Madame d'Auroučs came hurrying to the rescue and rated him soundly, threatening him with hell-fire and the Duchess's gibbet, and "the rascal was in such haste to descend that he thought to break his neck, and left his bonnet by the window."

They were cramped, too, in spite of the defection of three of their number. Jeanne Chevalier desired to return home, and no persuasion could prevail upon her to remain. Jeanne Brett wished to enter the Order of St. Benedict, and was transferred to the Convent of St. Menou. Antoinette Phelippon, on the death of her mother, went home to look after her little sisters.

Fearing that the delay occasioned by the building of the convent might result in the loss of further vocations, Father Gabriel-Maria and the Duchess gave all the postulants the choice of remaining where they were or transferring to other orders, should they find the period of waiting too long. All desired to remain, but each named the convent she would choose as an alternative, should the Duchess be unable to carry out her plans. They were reinforced, about this time, by a new postulant, Mathurine de Beaulieu. She was considerably senior to any of the others, and was a capable woman, a very welcome addition, as Joan found her able to undertake responsibility.

Preparations were made to build; and now at this point we meet with one of the most charming figures in Frances Guyard's narrative, George de Mannay, "Well-beloved George." He is actually the author of Chapter VIII of the Chronicle, the part which describes the building operations. George was one of the Duchess's gentlemen, her Master of the Horse, and he seems to have been her right-hand man. It was he who found the site, a slum area close to the palace and the city wall, occupied by gardens and houses of ill-fame; the property, scandalously enough, of the Chapter of Montermoyen. It was George who negotiated the sale; the canons wanted their price, and got it, eight hundred pieces of gold. He drew up the plans and supervised the building. When it came to the cutting of the first sods, a ceremonial affair with several ecclesiastical dignitaries taking part, it was Well-beloved George who handed the Duchess from her chair and put the little spade into her hand. Later on, when the convent was first occupied, we find him bustling about with fire-baskets, trying to get the place dried out, for it was very damp indeed when the sisters first took possession. It was always

George to whom they entrusted their little affairs. In spite of their deep affection for Joan, she always remained something of a royal personage, one to be held in awe, and not to be troubled with all the small concerns of life. With George, however, they stood on no such ceremony. He knew all their requirements. A word to him, and whatever was needful arrived.

He was a youngish man, this George de Mannay, at this time not forty years old. He had a wife who was afflicted with a deformity. "She is just as much deformed as I," Joan had observed during the Nullity Process, "and she has several lovely children."

There was a block of houses standing upon the new property, into which the postulants were transferred until such time as their convent should be ready to receive them. Here they were much more commodiously housed. They had a chapel, a refectory, a large dormitory and an infirmary, besides kitchen and other offices, and a room for Madame d'Aurouës, who continued to have charge of them.

It was in the latter half of the year 1502 that building operations began. Well-beloved George was sent, one morning, to invite the attendance of the Archbishop of Bourges and the Lord Abbot of St. Sulpice. When they arrived they found the place greatly improved. All the undesirable tenants had been cleared out, and the only occupants were the postulants in their new house. In place of a jumble of gardens and houses, there was now a broad stretch of green grass with a fine pear-tree growing in the middle. The Archbishop turned the first sod, the Abbot the next. Father Gabriel-Maria cut the third, and the Duchess had her turn, followed by the members of her household. Then the builders fell to work with great goodwill and zest. When evening came, and the site was deserted, there was a further little ceremony. Two by two, in complete silence, the postulants came out and took their share in the inauguration of the work. Each in turn dug a spadeful of earth; then, still in silence, they returned to the house.

In the spring of 1503 the foundation stones were laid, with the same ceremony, the same persons taking part. The plan was extremely simple, the buildings being arranged about three sides of a square. In the centre was the main block: to the right the offices, to the left the chapel. Then followed months of building. George de Mannay is at pains to recount the several incidents in which the workmen were protected, as by a miracle, from harm. Gradually the walls went up, the convent, the church.

The church still stands. It has unhappily been turned to profane use, and now serves as a military storehouse. The visitor to Bourges to-day may still see over the little arched doorway ten letters carved in stone, the initials of the Ten Virtues of Mary.

P	P	H	V	
L	O	P	P	
	P	L		(Lance)

Meanwhile another need was asserting itself. It was now two years since the little postulants had set out from Tours, with all their worldly possessions packed beside them into the wagons. They had grown since then and their clothes were becoming unwearable. They asked permission to send home for more. No, Madame said, that was her affair.

It was not a religious habit that she gave them, but it was at least a uniform: a dress of blue with white trimmings, and a white kerchief for the head. What could be more becoming for postulants of the Order of the blessed Virgin Mary? And now, as the twentieth of October 1502 drew near, their hearts beat fast with excitement and joy, for it was a great occasion, the clothing of the first five.

Father Gabriel-Maria sang the Mass, gave them Holy Communion, and preached the sermon. The five postulants knelt before Madame and begged the favour of the religious habit. One by one she took them aside and helped them to put on the grey robe—symbol of poverty which they shared with their sisters in the Franciscan Order: the red scapular, reminder of the love of Christ: the cord of ten knots, recalling the Ten Virtues. Their hair was shorn and their heads covered : veil of white for Mary's purity, ribbon of blue bearing her medal. Joan beheld her daughters kneeling before her, clad in the habit of penance surmounted by the royal colours red, white and blue, ancient livery of the house of Valois and subsequently of France, by centuries preceding the *tricoleur* of the Revolution.

The first to receive the habit was Mathurine de Beaulieu. The others were Marguerite Bodine, Marguerite Blandine, Marie Garelle, and Jeanne Jovere. Mathurine was to have been placed in charge, but her health broke down, and they were glad to find one to replace her in a Tertiary from Tours, Catherine Gauvinelle. The latter, though also of delicate health, was able to accomplish much by her mere presence and force of character. Her clothing took place on the fourth of November 1503, and from that time on she took charge of the community in the place of Madame d'Aurouës.

The months passed by, and the buildings began to approach completion; but the sisters were still in the same house when, on Whit Sunday, 1504, Joan sent in word that she was entertaining a large company to dinner, and would bring them over afterwards to see her daughters and hear the sermon. Accordingly she arrived with her guests, and was received by the sisters in the chapter-room. The Bishop of Albi was present, and also Madame de Linières. Father Gabriel-Maria preached the sermon; when it was over, the Duchess recommended her guests to the care of Catherine Gauvinelle and the other sisters, and withdrew with him into another room.

Nearly thirty years had gone by since the day when Joan, a young girl of twelve, had stood up beside an unwilling bridegroom and received from him the ring which was the symbol of their unhappy union. Now, kneeling at the feet of Father Gabriel-Maria, she plighted her troth to an Eternal Spouse. She took the three vows of religion, poverty, chastity, obedience. She added to them the vow of enclosure in a mitigated form, binding herself not to leave the town without permission.

The good father accepted her vows. "If you are

faithful to your promise," he said to her, "in place of the temporal spouse who has left you, you shall have one who will never abandon you, Jesus Christ our Saviour. He will give you his love for always, he will endow you with eternal life and the entire possession of himself."

She received a little silver ring which she set upon her finger to replace the royal ring which had brought her so little joy. Then Gabriel-Maria seated her in a chair, and in his turn knelt down and folded his hands between hers.

"I promise and vow," he said, "to God and the Virgin Mary and to you, Madame, that all my life I will keep the rule of the Virgin Mary, and all my life I will love her order and be faithful to it, and everywhere I will work for it."

In token of his affiliation to the order, Joan gave him a small scapular of scarlet cloth, which henceforth he wore always beneath his habit.

Transported with joy, Joan returned to laugh and talk with her children and the noble company. Then she took her guests away, and Father Gabriel-Maria told the sisters what had happened: that Madame had made her profession, the first religious of the Order of the Blessed Virgin Mary.

Greatly though she might desire it, Joan was not able to abandon the world altogether and enter into a convent, as many princesses have done. Two things prevented this: in the first place, God had given her charge of a duchy and her people needed her. It would never occur to her to abandon them. Secondly, she had undertaken to establish her order and secure her nuns from want, and this she could do only as long as she remained in possession of her income as Duchess of Berry, for apart from her revenues she was almost penniless. She could not afford to resign them.

In November of the same year the convent was completed, and the nuns made ready to move in. There was a series of clothing ceremonies, for Joan wished that all should have the habit before entering into the enclosure. During the past two years there had been a steady inflow of postulants. They now numbered twenty-one in all.

Prior to their taking possession of the new convent, the first five were admitted to profession. This was on the ninth of November, when Catherine Gauvinelle, Frances de Mohet, Marguerite Bodine, Marguerite Blandine and Marie Garelle took the vows of religion and received the large veil and scapular and the mantle of white. On the finger of each was placed the ring of espousal. Catherine Gauvinelle, as "Mère Ancelle," received a gold ring in addition. As the novices chanted the *Te Deum*, the Duchess took them in her arms and kissed them on the lips, all except one, Marguerite Blandine, who—revealing detail—was ill of fever, and contented herself with kissing the Duchess's hand.

Then Father Gabriel-Maria announced to them the privileges to which their profession entitled them. For the next ten days they would observe complete silence, the "bridal silence", devoting themselves entirely to Christ their Spouse. On each of those days they might receive him in Holy Communion. Further, he told them, the Sovereign Pontiff had accorded them the privilege of nominating each ten spiritual friends, men or women, who should participate in all the merits and good works of the order, present and to come.

Frances de Mohet, the second of the five, was the Duchess's young maid-of-honour. Joan held her in great affection, and used to call her "my Beline" (my Baa-Lamb). An orphan, without father or mother, her only relative being a brother, she was a gifted, intelligent girl of fourteen, very wealthy, with thoughts and tastes all for worldly things. Joan and her holy director had devoted much time to persuasion, and still more to prayer; for the maid's gifts were such that it was well seen that she would make a notable religious. All their efforts seemed to be in vain. Frances had a good will to serve and please God, but in the world. The life of a nun held no attraction for her. Father Gabriel-Maria made a final effort to draw her to God, and even as she was attempting to answer him, she experienced within herself a sudden entire change of heart. "Father," she cried out, "I will do everything to please Madame and you. If she will be pleased to put me among her daughters in religion, she will be doing me great honour." After that there was no desire to turn back.

The day that Frances received the habit, the Duchess invited all the Court to witness the ceremony, and bade them put on their best attire, as if it were a wedding they were attending. She herself was wearing her most splendid robe of cramoisy velvet. The secret had been well kept. Until the actual ceremony none knew the identity of the little postulant to be received. There were gasps and exclamations of wonder when they saw who it was upon whom Madame was putting the holy habit. There were those among them who would have hindered her if they could, but it was too late now. Frances was safe in the arms of Mary.

Such was the vocation of Frances de Mohet, destined to be one of the shining lights of the order.

At last the great day approached when the nuns were to enter into their convent, and close the door for ever upon the world and its distractions. They had long been looking forward to this day. Now, on November the 21st, their long deferred desire was to be granted.

The previous day Madame sent the crier round to make proclamation that if any wished to see the sisters, they must do so at once, for to-morrow they would enter the enclosure.

The date had been carefully chosen. It was the feast of the Presentation of the Virgin Mary. Joan and Gabriel-Maria, like holy Anne and Joachim, prepared that day to bring their daughters into the Temple of God and offer them up to his service.

When the day came, Joan was astir at a very early hour. She had slept little that night, "for, notwithstanding she was couched in bed, her spirit waked and was with God in prayer." She heard Mass and received Holy Communion; afterwards, in company with her household, she repaired to the church.

The nave was partitioned into two parts. In the front half the public were accommodated; the back was designed to be the choir of the brothers of the order. Such brothers had been a part of Joan's scheme from the first. They were to attend to the spiritual needs of the sisters and be their connecting link with the outside world. The sisters' tribune was a gallery situated immediately above the brothers' choir, and it was entered by a stairway communicating with the convent.

The church was packed with people. All the townsfolk were there, anxious to show their appreciation of the Duchess and of the good work she had taken in hand. The front seats were assigned to Monsieur and Madame d'Aumont and the other ladies and gentlemen of the Court. The brothers' choir, at present vacant, was used to accommodate the congregation.

The Duchess and Father Gabriel-Maria took their seats in the sisters' choir, and Fathers Girard and Ambrose were sent to summon the nuns. Walking two and two, with joined hands and downcast eyes, they came, passing into their own garden and up the stairs into their choir: fifteen steps there were, to commemorate the fifteen steps which Mary mounted coming into the Temple at Jerusalem. As the people waited in the church they heard the sound of voices coming nearer. They were singing *In exitu Israel de Egypto*. They entered the tribune. Madame spoke, making the gift of "her soul, her body, and these her daughters, present and to come, to God and his holy Mother; also of the church and convent which she had built to their honour." Sister Catherine Gauvinelle replied for the nuns, humbly thanking the Duchess for the honour she had done them, and accepting the donation which she was offering them. One by one Joan conducted the sisters to their stalls. Catherine Gauvinelle as "Mère Ancelle" was placed in the first stall on the right, with Marguerite Blandine her Assistant on the left. The others were ranged in their places. The professed sisters put on the white cloaks which they were to wear in choir. The grille facing the altar had been left wide open, so that for this, the last time, the crowds in the church were able to look in and see the earnest young faces, turned towards the high altar in jubilation and thankfulness. The people were not slow to avail themselves of the opportunity, standing up on the benches in order to see better.

High Mass began. The celebrant was the venerable Archbishop of Bourges, William de Cambray, who had taken an active and interested part at every stage of the inauguration of the Order and the building of the church. After the *Domine non sum dignus*, the congregation beheld a strange sight. The stairway leading up to the grille in the nuns' choir was not yet completed, and to give them Holy Communion the Archbishop was obliged to mount a ladder. He was an old man of eighty; accordingly two other ladders were brought, and the deacon and sub-deacon mounted with him, supporting him on either side.

The ceremony was followed by a little love-feast at which Madame presided, with Father Gabriel-Maria on her right, and on her left, Catherine Gauvinelle, the first "Mère Ancelle"—Mother Handmaid, humblest and most pleasing of Mary's titles, henceforth always borne by the Superioress. It was a long time before Joan could tear herself away. At length she passed out through the gateway communicating with the palace. The door was shut. The nuns turned the key and went back into their own house.

The Order of the Virgin Mary, conceived in a child's heart so many weary years ago, had grown to a full and glorious maturity. That same devoted heart now remained behind the grille, as Joan came sadly away, to accomplish in patience the task which God had given her.

CHAPTER XI

THE ORDER OF PEACE

AS the Christmas of 1504 drew near, Joan could look back on six years of freedom: six years during which she had been, in a sense, her own mistress, free to regulate her affairs, dispose of her property, and occupy herself according to her own pleasure. We have seen in the preceding chapters the kind of use she made of her freedom. Her time, her energies, and her purse had been devoted to the needs of her subjects and the foundation of her order. She had accepted the responsibility of her duchy and carried out, with conscientiousness and charity, the duties which it entailed. She had given her daughters the peace of the enclosure, a peace denied to herself. Last of all, she had made an oblation to God of all the liberty so painfully acquired, when at the feet of her director she took the vows of religion.

A nun, yet of the world: a duchess, living under vow! Only by the inspiration and the special grace of God could such a thing be. To save one's soul under either state alone is as much as most people can do.

Speaking of Joan to her nuns the day after her death, Gabriel-Maria revealed some of her qualities which were known to him alone. She was so humble, he told them, that she would invent opportunities for humiliation, and compel him, under the pact they had made together, to apply to her all the terms she could think of that would most wound her pride: "haughty," "hunch-backed," "deformed." "I would offer her humiliations," he said, "such as I would not impose upon a novice. For my own part, often I was abashed that she could endure all the things I said to her."

He spoke, too, of her prudence. She never gave an answer without first consulting God and our blessed Lady. People would come to her for advice on affairs of the greatest moment, so convinced were they that her decisions were of God. "She was righteous and true," he said, "doing justice to all men, great and small alike. . . . Her whole pleasure was to pray to God, and to have him always in her heart, on her tongue, and in her works."

It is obvious, therefore, that during these years of activity and endeavour, there must have been an ever-deepening sense of intimacy with God which only prayer could bring. Some of her devotions we have noted, in particular her burning love for Christ Crucified, and in the Blessed Sacrament of the Altar. She would shed tears of contrition and love as she received him in Holy Communion: and if we are to believe the words of the chronicler, she was favoured, a century before St. Margaret Mary, with a revelation of the Sacred Heart.

"One time," Frances Guyard tells us, "the holy lady was greatly desirous that her heart should be wholly one with that of Jesus our Saviour: and as she contemplated the love which he had shown her in becoming man and dying on the cross for her, she did languish of her great desire and could neither eat nor drink. Her servants came to tell the reverend father that she was ill: and he laughed, for he knew well what manner of malady it was of which she suffered. When she had these spiritual consolations, all the world was naught to her."

Father Gabriel-Maria came and questioned her, and after much hesitation she answered him: "Father, I have been bidden to-morrow to a banquet."

The following morning he said Mass in her chapel and then left her in prayer. She remained there so long that her people grew anxious and came at last and brought her out to dinner. She ate in a sort of trance, not knowing what she was doing. Later on, when she was able to speak, Gabriel-Maria questioned her again, "Madame, tell me of the banquet which Jesus has given you."

Joan related to him how she had been entertained by our Lord and his holy Mother at a feast, at which two hearts were presented to her, and our Lady bade her take and eat. Afterwards Jesus asked for her heart in return. She put her hand to her breast but could not find it there, at which she was greatly distressed; but Jesus looked upon her very lovingly.

Her heart was gone, Gabriel-Maria told the chronicler, because Christ had already taken it and united it with his own. It is a narration in simple, symbolic terms of a love unifying and transforming, a state amounting to the mystical marriage which we recognise from the similar experience of other saints.

The devotion of Joan to our blessed Lady was a natural consequence of the love she bore to Christ. She knew no better way to honour him than by venerating and imitating the one whom he loves above all others. This devotion, as we have seen, led her to devise and follow out a rule of life which is nothing less than an imitation in detail of the life and virtues of Mary.

She had a favourite prayer to our blessed Lady, which may be translated thus:

O Mary, Jesus' Mother sweet,
Make me your handmaid true;
And give me grace, in all my days,
To be in grace with you.
Grant me to love the ones I love,
Because of their love for you;
And my love for you be the reason why
They come to love me too.

Mention has been made of the papal privilege by virtue of which each religious might nominate ten persons to be affiliated to the order and share in its merits. With a like intention Joan planned that each convent should have ten persons as protectors, who should participate in the good works of the house. It was for her daughters and for these associates and protectors that she obtained the indulgence of the "Devotion of the Ten Ave Marias."

One day, after Gabriel-Maria had returned from Rome with the approved Rule, the Duchess called her daughters about her and said to them, "Children, our holy Father the Pope has granted me an indulgenced prayer to give to whomever I wish. It is the *Devotion of the Ten Ave Marias*, and it is to be recited in honour of the Ten Virtues of the glorious Virgin Mary. You are the first to receive it."

It was a little rosary which she gave them, consisting of one large and ten small beads. On the large bead was said the Our Father for the intentions of the Pope; on each of the small beads, the Hail Mary. After the words "Holy Mary, Mother of God," was inserted an invocation commemorating each Virtue in turn, thus:

Holy Mary, Mother of God, Virgin most pure, pray for us, etc.

Holy Mary, Mother of God, Virgin most prudent, pray for us, etc.

Holy Mary, Mother of God, Virgin most humble, pray for us, etc.

Holy Mary, Mother of God, Virgin most faithful, pray for us, etc.

Holy Mary, Mother of God, Virgin most devout, pray for us, etc.

Holy Mary, Mother of God, Virgin most obedient, pray for us, etc.

Holy Mary, Mother of God, Virgin most poor, pray for us, etc.

Holy Mary, Mother of God, Virgin most patient, pray for us, etc.

Holy Mary, Mother of God, Virgin most charitable, pray for us, etc.

Holy Mary, Mother of God, Virgin most sorrowful, pray for us, etc.

This indulgence of the Ten Ave Marias which the nuns were privileged to give to their friends led to the formation of bands of associates, all joining in the devotion to Mary's Virtues, and all sharing in the spiritual benefits of the Order. They became known as the Second Order of the Virgin Mary, a term which implied no more than a privileged confraternity. One charming practice recommended to them was the recitation, day and night, of the Hail Mary each time they heard the clock strike.

We come now to the third of the Orders which Joan of France established, the *Order of Peace*.

It is not too much to claim for our saint that she was, from birth, dedicated to the cause of peace. We have seen how, an infant in arms, she was made partner in an alliance calculated to bring peace to the kingdom. Her father was a man of peace, a tireless worker for the unity of France, never drawing the sword until every other means had failed. It was he who gave orders that daily at midday the Hail Mary should be said "for the peace and union of the realm," and who obtained from the Pope an indulgence of three hundred days for each recital. Joan had lent herself loyally to her father's designs for peace. Throughout her unhappy married life she had striven to restrain and reconcile her rebellious husband. In her later years she came to realize that peace is a matter, not of human alliances and treaties, not of diplomacy and scheming, but of the conversion of hearts to God: the building up of a strong host of ordinary people in whom the love of God comes first, and the love of one's neighbour next. Only when the earth is inhabited by men and women animated by such a spirit of charity, will peace come to reign upon it.

She lived her life in a world torn by war, riddled by factions, rotten with intrigue. She had dwelt in the centre of it, seen the lack of faith, the envy, jealousy and hatred that result from self-seeking; the beast that man becomes as soon as he averts his eyes from God. Brave, resolute and chaste, she sought the only way to oppose these evils: to love God with her whole heart, and influence others to love him too.

The origin of her Order of Peace Gabriel-Maria ascribes to a colloquy between her and our blessed Lady. "My daughter," our Lady said to her, "there are three things which delight me exceedingly. On earth, my first joy was to hear Jesus speak. In order that I might miss no word of his discourse, I followed him to Galilee and wherever else he went, in company with the other women. My second devotion was the contemplation of his Passion, his Cross and each of his Wounds. My third was a great love of the Sacrament of the Altar, and the Holy Mass. You too, my daughter, if you practise these three devotions, cannot fail to be dear to me and to my Son."

Later on our Lady gave her a further explanation. "With regard to the first," she said, "in your conversation you should always be kind to everyone, and exert yourself to bring peace to reign among those with whom you dwell. If you see anyone commit sin, set yourself to pray for him, that you may save his soul."

"The second point," our Lady went on, "concerns

the Wounds of my Son. Every morning you will make a resolution to meditate upon these Divine Wounds and you will desire during the day to endure some suffering for love of my Son.

"The third point refers to the Sacrifice and Sacrament of the Altar. You will honour this Sacrament by hearing Mass every day as far as you are able."

Love of one's neighbour, the cultivation of peace, meditation upon the Passion of Our Lord, a great devotion to the Blessed Sacrament, these were the particular points on which Joan was to concentrate. These were the devotions which she was to implant in the hearts of those whom she united in the Order of Peace.

This Order, the Third Order instituted by Joan of France, is not a Third Order in the commonly accepted sense of the term. Benedictines, Franciscans, Dominicans all have their First, Second and Third Orders: the First for monks, the Second for nuns, and the Third for laymen and women living in the world. A Third Order is a definite Order of the Church, with a rule, a habit, an Office, and a noviciate preceding profession. The members, while pursuing the ordinary avocations of their state of life, are able at the same time to live in the spirit and enjoy the privileges of the First and Second Orders to which they are attached. No one can be a member of more than one of these. A person can not be a Dominican, for instance, and a Franciscan too.

The Order of Peace stands in a different category. In its constitution it is more like a Confraternity, and its members are drawn from Catholics of all ranks, clerical, religious, and lay. Its end is to work for the glory of God by the sanctification of its members, and to foster among all men the spirit of charity, the Peace of Christ.

The rules of the Order are embodied in the following points as taught by the Bl. Father Gabriel-Maria.

The first is a regulation for the *heart*: "The Brothers and Sisters of the Order can not and must not have in their heart any hatred, rancour or ill-will against anyone whatsoever; nor may they harbour any desire or inclination for revenge even on their enemies; but they must pardon their fellow-creatures for the love of Christ."

The second refers to the *tongue*: "The Brothers and Sisters of the Order must never speak ill of anyone whatsoever; rather they must make excuses for those persons of whom evil is spoken."

The third concerns *actions*: "The Brothers and Sisters of the Order must exert themselves to make peace between those who are involved in quarrels, contentions, strifes and feuds."

It would be a different world if all men and women were faithful to these precepts. There would be no sins of the heart, no envy or covetousness, no class-hatred: nor of the tongue, no malicious talk, no evil propaganda: nor of action, no strifes or quarrels, no wars. Each person, loving Christ, would behold in his neighbour only the image of the Loved One; for Peace is Love, the choicest outpouring of the Holy Spirit.

"Send forth thy Spirit, and our hearts shall be

regenerated, And thou shalt renew the face of the earth."

Peace: Love. The badge of the Order of Peace displays a Cross bearing the inscription: Pax, Caritas, so:

  C
PAX
  R
  I
  T
  A
  S

It also shows the emblems of the Holy Eucharist, the Sword of the Word of God, and the initials A.M. (Ave Maria.)

The Order of Peace imposes no obligations binding under sin. It recommends its member to be faithful to the spirit of Peace, to attend Mass and receive Holy Communion as frequently as possible, and to recite daily the *Triple Crown*, which is an extension of the Devotion of the Ten Ave Marias.

The Triple Crown is a rosary which fulfils the three special devotions recommended by our Lady to Joan. It is composed of three parts. On each of the ten *white* beads is recited the Hail Mary with the special invocation commemorating each virtue in turn; on each of the five *red* beads, the Our Father for love of the five Wounds of Christ and the Hail Mary in memory of the five principal sorrows of Mary; on each of the twelve *black* beads a Hail Mary in thanksgiving for the twelve fruits of the Holy Spirit, bestowed upon those who have devotion to the Blessed Sacrament of the Altar. There are three large beads in addition, on which the Our Father is recited for the intentions of the Pope and the peace of the Church : the first in memory of our Lord's love for souls, the second in memory of all he has suffered for them, and the third in memory of all that he has merited for them.

Such is the Triple Crown, the instrument which Joan of France and Gabriel-Maria put into the hands of the host of men and women whom they gathered together, under the title of the Order of Peace, four and a half centuries ago. Their object was to bring peace to a world distracted with war, in which the charity of Christ was growing cold. It was to grow colder still. In their own day, did they but know it, a movement was to be set on foot to cast down Mary from her throne. Her shrines, adorned by the piety of generations, were to be sacked and looted; her images hacked to pieces or burnt; her name removed from liturgies. If she were remembered at all, it would be as some necessary accidental, of little more importance than the ass or the ox that shared their stable with her. And the inevitable happened. As surely as it is impossible to have a baby without a mother, so forgetting the Mother men also forgot the Child who was the Redeemer of the world.

Four centuries ago: and all that time Mary has never ceased to plead, to beg mercy for those who "know not what they do." Now, in our own day, we see the glimmering of better things to come. Slowly, surely, her prayers—the prayers which God has willed and asked for—are being granted. The Church of

Christ is entering upon a new phase, with saintly Popes, a zealous and enlightened clergy, and a people torn and ravaged by unbelief and disorder, but at the same time strengthened and enriched by the heroic endurance of a glorious and daily increasing army of martyrs.

Here and there, amid this awakening out of chaos, Mary gives us a glimpse of herself. Now it is a peasant girl of Lourdes who receives the message: "Repent: do penance." Now three little children at Fatima are bidden to *pray*—pray and offer sacrifice for the conversion of sinners. Now it is the Sovereign Pontiff's inspiration to consecrate the universal Church to Mary's Immaculate Heart. Now it is the springing into existence of an army of men and women all over the world, the very counterpart of Joan's army, who aim to imitate Mary and thereby *show her to the world.*[1] Last of all, it is the raising to the altars of the Church of such lovers of Mary as Bernadette, Louis Marie de Montfort—and Joan of France.

[1] The Legion of Mary.

CHAPTER XII

LAST DAYS

"BEFORE thy death thou shalt found an Order in honour of me," was the promise made by our Lady to Joan of France. The Order was now founded and the Rule approved. The convent was built: the nuns established there under their *Mère Ancelle*. The last step had been taken on November the 21st, 1504, when Joan inducted her daughters into their convent and left them in the security of the enclosure.

"Before thy death. . . ." On that day in November when she set her nuns in their stalls and conducted them to their cells, only two and a half months of life remained to her. To such delicate and precise margins does God work.

Christmas was a happy time. In the first year of their coming to Bourges she had given her daughters the gift of a Crib. It was a devotion very dear to her, the child of St. Francis, the saint who originated this method of presenting, in vivid form, the drama of Bethlehem, the mystery of the Incarnation. During these days it was her great delight to come to visit them, waiting humbly for admission at the door which communicated with the palace, of which the nuns always had the key.

"She would sit herself down in the chair which still stands at the fireside," Frances Guyard tells us, "and watch them busy at their tasks, and she would disport herself with them so familiarly that it would seem as though they were her own daughters."

She was very anxious in those last days—for it looks as though she was aware of her approaching end—that there should be no relaxation of the early fervour.

"One day it happened by accident that in passing through the dormitory, she found one who was breaking the silence at the door of her room. She chided her with so marvellous a vehemence as to make all the others tremble: so much so that the Reverend Father had a great ado to calm her. And she said to him, 'Father, let me correct them. If they commit such faults in my presence, what will it be after my death? Is this to be a relaxed Order?' "

Frances Guyard adds lovingly that Madame and the Reverend Father made much of little faults "for fear that they should fall into greater ones. And they did right, for our Saviour had called these first ones to be an example to all those who should come after them."

The Duchess welcomed every excuse for giving presents to her daughters. She brought them some of the relics of her grandeur, the cloth of gold that had been her wedding-train, the dress of cramoisy velvet which she had worn on state occasions, another dress of black velvet. These were to be converted into vestments. Mother Catherine Gauvinelle had them made up and embroidered at Madame's expense.

On New Year's Day she had presents, little pictures, for all the nuns. She had already seen to it that in every part of the convent they should have a reminder of the sacred mystery of the Annunciation, the titular dedication of the convent. It was represented in bas-relief over the door of the choir for the brothers; around it were carved the initials of the Ten Virtues painted in blue and gold. The big stained-glass window behind the high altar showed the same scene, and represented in addition the Duchess presenting her daughters and her convent to the Blessed Virgin. Over the high altar was a beautiful carving in stone of the same subject, coloured and gilded. It was the same in every other part of the convent.

The great bell too: Joan had it cast and adorned with representations of the Crucifix and the Annunciation. Upon it were engraved the words:

Joan of France named me,
And to Mary gave me.

The bell was solemnly blessed, "baptised" in the name of *Mary*, and set up soon after the completion of the convent. Joan did not live to see the mounting of the second bell, *Gabriel*.

The feast of the Epiphany was the occasion of further gifts. Madame put into the hands of Mother Catherine Gauvinelle ten pieces of gold bearing the device of the Annunciation.

"And the holy lady said to them: 'Children, gold

is the symbol of charity. Always remember to love God above all things. Keep him always in mind, all that you do, do for love of him. If you so act, never shall you be separated from him, neither in this world nor in the next. You must love your neighbour too and all your sisters, doing them the good that in reason you would have them do to you, never doing aught to them that you would not wish them to do to you.

" 'I give you also incense. It is the symbol of prayer, fragrant before the face of God. It signifies that you must love to worship God and devote yourselves above all things to prayer, if you wish to advance in virtue and the love of God. Prayer is the chief activity in which I would have you occupy your whole life, for which I have placed you here in the Order of the Virgin Mary.'

"And for myrrh, Madame gave them her little discipline, bidding them be ever mindful of the scourging and all the bitter sufferings which sweet Jesus endured in his Passion."

She was with them again four days later, on the 10th of January, when she made her will in the convent, writing it in her own hand, a sister holding the desk for her:

> "In the Name of God and of the Virgin Mary. I, Joan of France, Duchess of Berry, being sound in mind and body, make this the testament and disposition of my last will as follows, seeing that it is more to the pleasure of God and the good of my soul to do it now than to defer it and wait until

death: and for the same reason, that I may please God and save my soul, it is my intention during my lifetime to carry out my dispositions, as far as I may be able to do so.

"I bequeath my soul to God and the Virgin Mary and I appoint my burial-place to be in the church of my Order of the Virgin Mary founded by me in my city of Bourges: and I will that it be within the Sisters' choir, to the end that they may pray often for me."

She named as her heirs her sister, Anne de Bourbon, and the daughter of the latter, with a first charge upon the estate of a yearly income sufficient to secure the needs of the convent. She remembered all the members of her household, and made a long list of charities which were to receive legacies. She also bequeathed large sums to be expended in Masses for the repose of her soul. At the end she signed her name for the last time : "Jehanne de France."

On the feast of St. Vincent, January the 22nd, Joan came in to the convent and seemed distressed regarding some arrangement in connection with a special sermon. She was obviously very ill, complaining of pain in her heart and agonising toothache, and begged the nuns to pray for her. As she came out through the little garden gate, she turned and gave orders for it to be walled up the following day. She would not need it again, she said.

There was sad grief in the convent when Father Gabriel-Maria came to tell the nuns that Madame had taken to her bed. They began to storm Heaven with prayers and penances for her recovery; but Gabriel-Maria gave them no hope of that. As he was saying his Mass, he told them, he had seen, standing at the corner of the altar, a vision of one whom he had known and venerated on earth, a dear friend to himself and to Joan, the venerable Jean de la Fontaine, her first confessor. The holy man had foretold her death in ten days' time. Gabriel-Maria could scarcely speak for weeping, and the sisters were no less affected.

Meanwhile Joan was getting worse, and the pain was so intense that she could not sleep at all. She made her confession and received Holy Communion, and now Gabriel-Maria came to her for their last talk together.

Her injunctions to him, given in her hour of weakness and pain, were written down and included in the Chronicle under the title of the "Little Testament." As she lay there dying, we can see that her mind was wandering back over the years, and that she was gathering together for his benefit and the benefit of her Order, the fruits of her own bitter experience.

"Father, I beg you, never have the desire or the will to wait upon the Court. I know it better than you. . . .

"Meddle not with the marriage of any, no matter how good the person, for often these things turn out differently from what one looked for. . . .

"Take no part in Court affairs, unless it be in matters spiritual or for the saving of souls. . . .

"Have no wish to be bishop or prelate of the Church. If they bring pressure to bear, refuse, as you have always done hitherto.

"Have no concern with worldly men or their affairs: and know well who it is to whom you declare your heart. Put not your faith in all men. . . .

"Do not credit the great, nor others either, when they speak ill of anyone. Always observe, and bid my sisters observe, the precept which you have given me, ever to make excuse for those of whom evil is spoken.

"Use with others greater diligence than you have used with me, in exhorting them to well-doing, for I have been slothful, and I do repent me now.

"Above all, and as my last word, I implore you, see that my sisters keep the rule and statutes which I have given them. Let them not cease to observe them, nor seek relaxation of them. Let them preserve always the stairways of purity and charity.

"Father, I leave my sisters in your keeping. Do not ever abandon them, and do not forget me, when I am dead. I have told you all this . . . it is my last testament . . . my farewell to you and to my sisters. They must not be grieved at my death . . . their good Mother will keep and defend them, and they will have enough. . . .

"Father . . . I know that I am going to die and must render my account before God: but I trust that the Virgin Mary will be my defence."

Gabriel-Maria promised her then that he would watch faithfully over the Order, and be its father and friend always: and he begged her in turn that when she should be with God and his holy Mother, she would commend to them her orphaned children and himself.

Candlemas came, and Joan began to lose ground rapidly. She could retain no food and was unable to receive Holy Communion. On the vigil of the feast, her children in the convent fasted with her on bread and water, and prayers were offered on her behalf in all the churches and convents in the city: "for she was loved of all of them." On February the 4th the great bell of St. Stephen's began to toll, and the people, sad at heart, knelt down and joined in prayer for the Good Duchess.

Father Gabriel-Maria scarcely left her. He was looking so stricken and weary that Madame gently begged him to go to bed. She would send for him, she said, if she got any worse. When he had gone she dismissed all the rest, keeping by her only her waiting women.

She must have mentioned to them, for they remembered it afterwards, that when her mother Charlotte was dying, there was such a noise and tumult around her that her poor head was all bewildered, and she could not recollect herself, to prepare for death. Joan desired that it might not be so with her. She prayed that in her last moments she might have peace and quiet to make ready to meet her Lord. She bade them turn her to the far side of the bed, draw the curtains, and take away the light. They obeyed. All withdrew, excepting Marie Pot, who quietly placed herself where she could see through the curtains.

So she sat for an hour crouched in the dark, without a sound except the breathing of the dying woman.

Suddenly it seemed to her that the bed was full of light. She turned round, thinking someone had come in with a torch, but the room was in darkness. She looked back through the curtains, and there was the light, resting over the figure of her mistress.

The circle of light grew narrower : crept upwards, to the breast, to the mouth: went out. Marie Pot pulled back the curtains, and bent down. There was no movement, no breath. Joan of France was dead.

Over in the church of the Annonciade the nuns waited. It was long past their hour for retiring, but no one thought of going to bed. They knelt and prayed. Presently the night was rent with shrieks and lamentations, coming from the palace opposite. Then they heard the boom of the great bell, tolling the passing. There was a knock at the gate, and Well-beloved George came in to tell them what they had already guessed, that Madame had passed away that night at ten o'clock.

They began to sing Matins; but the thought of their loss was more than they could bear. One after another the sisters broke down and choked on the words, until at last only one voice remained singing steadily on. It was the voice of Frances de Mohet. She, who knew Joan best of all of them, and loved her most dearly, had inherited something of her steely strength and self-control. Gradually peace came to the others; and when they stood up to chant *Te Deum Laudamus*, it seemed to them as though a radiant Presence stole in and stood among them, singing praise to God.

CHAPTER XIII

THE LEGACY OF JOAN OF FRANCE

IT was Shrove Tuesday, Carnival day, when Joan died. Normally the streets would have been alive with revelry and excitement. To-night all was quiet and subdued. "There was none could eat nor drink for the great sorrow in which they were; for high and low, rich and poor, loved her, and not without cause."

The women set to work to prepare her for burial; they discovered the haircloth, the iron chain she was wearing. Then the body was embalmed, and clothed in the habit of a professed nun of the Order. Enclosed in three shells it lay in state in the Great Hall of the palace, and there Masses were said for eighteen days in its presence.

On the eve of the funeral the body was removed to the Grande Chapelle, and vigil kept there all through the night. It was a scene of magnificence. The immense chandelier, holding a hundred and sixty candles, which had not been in use since the occasion of the consecration of the church, was lit again in honour of the Good Duchess.

On the morrow the solemn Requiem was sung, and all the bells in the city began to toll as the funeral procession moved off from the palace gates. Four noblemen held a canopy over the coffin, which was surmounted by an effigy of the saint, clothed in the habit and wearing the ducal crown. It was borne along on a litter carried by black-trapped mules, with little bells that tinkled upon their harness. At the head of the procession walked the clergy: the Cardinal of Bourbon, archbishops, bishops, monks and priests, a contingent from every church in Bourges. On either side of the coffin were the ladies and gentlemen of the household, and behind it the chief mourner, Monsieur de Bourbon, Anne's son-in-law, followed by all the notabilities of the city, then a train of scholars, widows and orphans, the poor and infirm; and mourning crowds lined the streets through which they passed.

The nuns of the Annonciade, sitting close to the grille, saw the coffin of their beloved mother borne up to the high altar. Close to it followed Father Gabriel-Maria: looking, they thought, more dead than alive. After the funeral rites had been performed the coffin was lowered into the vault and the iron grating closed. Sadly the mourners filed past the tomb to take their farewell. The last glimpse of the scene which Frances Guyard gives us is of one of the Duchess's gentlemen casting down his staff by the grating, with a bitter cry: "Oh, my Mistress, my kind Mistress, I shall never serve you again! Oh, pray for me!"

The death of a saint, however dearly loved and regretted, is not a matter for sadness. The natural sorrow which it occasions soon gives place to other emotions. So it was with Joan. Almost immediately her people began to realize that their Duchess, happy in the sight of God, was far more potent to relieve their needs than she had ever been while still among them. Once again, and regretfully, for it is our last meeting with him, we quote from the chronicle the words of George de Mannay:

"She had a gardener named Sire Mathurin, who was ill of the gout in his arms, his legs and his whole body, so much so that he could not budge from his bed, nor turn nor lift himself without aid: and he suffered extreme pain night and day. He had a lodging in the house of Master Nicolle Barry, in an upper room that looked upon the street which runs from Montermoyen to the palace.

"And after the death of Madame, the day she was entombed in the church of the Annonciade, she was carried from the palace to the said church, in company with a procession from all the churches in Bourges. And as they carried her by, the said Master Mathurin, lying in his bed in great misery and pain, heard the procession singing. And he, greatly troubled, began to cry out, 'My good Mistress, I shall never see you again'. And he called to the captain de Maubranche, named Jeannou, husband of La Bergenine, who was seated at the window of the said Master Mathurin, and said to him, 'Oh my friend, come and help me to drag myself to the window, for I wish to see my good Mistress.' The which aided him with great labour to fetch himself to the window. And he had on naught but his shirt and his gown.

"And when he saw my Lady pass, he fell on his knees and begged her, if she had power with God, that she would pray for her poor servant who was left without mistress, and powerless in his limbs. And after he had made his prayer, he did not quit the window, but watched all the mourners pass. And when everyone was gone past, the captain came to take hold of him and fetch him back to his bed, and suddenly he said to him, 'Captain, good friend, let me be, for I feel I am cured, thanks to our Lord, and by the prayers of my good lady and mistress.' And incontinent he began to leap, and unaided did on his shoes and doublet as well as ever he had done."

The captain ran off to the palace to tell what had happened, and George was sent to see Mathurin, and so had the story from his own lips.

This was the first of many such occurrences. In the days which followed and on throughout the years, there was a constant stream of sufferers of all kinds coming to Bourges to invoke the aid of the Good Duchess. Soon the walls of the church were covered with ex-voto offerings. The anniversary of her death, February 4th, was observed yearly as a special festival, and she was invoked as one of the patrons of the city. Less than twenty years after she died, an Office in her honour was celebrated in Bourges. Her cult was spontaneous, springing into being out of the hearts of the people who loved her and revered her memory.

Meanwhile the Annonciade remained. In spite of

the heavy blow it had sustained in the death of the foundress, at a time when the convent was barely built and many necessaries were still lacking, it went on, under the protection of Anne de Bourbon, and the care of Madame d'Aumont.

Even so, difficulties arose. The Franciscan friars, Ambrose Basset and Girard Pasquet, were withdrawn, and in October 1506, only eighteen months after the death of Joan, we find the nuns appealing to the King's minister, George of Amboise, for someone to be appointed to visit them and see to their spiritual needs. In consequence of this appeal, Friar Ambrose Basset was returned to the Annonciade by the Minister Provincial of Touraine.

Joan had foreseen this difficulty, and had intended to forestall it when she designed to make the Order of the Blessed Virgin a mixed order. There were to be brothers who should attend to the spiritual needs of the nuns, and at the same time act as missioners among the people, preaching devotion to Mary and the imitation of her virtues as the surest way of pleasing and serving Jesus Christ her Son. Joan planned to have brothers in considerable numbers. This is evident from the fact that the choir she built for them was of equal dimensions with that of the sisters; and there are various indications that during her lifetime a certain number of brothers were received and were living in the special building prepared for them.

In the original Rule, approved on February 12th, 1502, by Pope Alexander VI, the sisters are placed under the obedience of Father Gilbert Nicholas

(Gabriel-Maria) "until such time as the brothers shall be introduced into the said convents." Privileges are granted to "the Sisters and Brothers *already received*," and the habit for the brothers is prescribed, with the three colours and the capuche. Again, in her will, Joan refers to the habit and office of clerical and lay brothers respectively.

It seems probable, however, that owing to the premature death of the foundress, the recruitment of men into the Order was never prosecuted, and ceased at an early date; and of those already received, none ever became competent to undertake the direction of the nuns.

In January 1507 the Rule was approved anew by Pope Julius II, probably at the instance of Anne of Bourbon, as executrix of her sister's will. The Bull granted to Anne the personal privilege of nominating as director for the Order any person she should deem suitable, to be selected either from a reformed congregation of one of the four Mendicant Orders, or from the Benedictines of St. Sulpice or from any other community of St. Benedict or St. Bernard. The Bull also referred to "the Sisters and Brothers at present living enclosed in the convent of the Order."

By this Bull the direction of the Order of the Blessed Virgin Mary was conferred provisionally upon the nominee of Anne of Bourbon. A few months later Anne wrote to Father John Sauvage, Vicar General of the Cismontine Observants, requesting his Order to undertake the direction of the Annonciade.

It looks as though Anne still hoped that at some future time the spiritual needs of the order might be met by its own brothers, but this never came to pass; and when, on the 20th July, 1517, the definitive Rule, drawn up by Gabriel-Maria, was approved by Pope Leo X, the Annonciade was placed definitely under the obedience of the Franciscans of the Observance, and this arrangement remained in force for many generations. To-day each convent is under the jurisdiction of the Ordinary of the diocese, by whom the appointment of the spiritual director is made.

It was Louis of Amboise the younger, Bishop of Albi, who was responsible for the second convent of the Order, founded at Albi in 1507. Catherine Gauvinelle was transferred as first Mère Ancelle, and with her seven other Sisters, including Marguerite Blandine and Marie Bodine. The new community flourished and attracted many vocations. In 1512 Catherine Gauvinelle and Marguerite Blandine were able to return to Bourges.

The third convent was that of Bruges, founded in 1517, at the request of Margaret of Austria, who had always maintained a warm affection and regard for Joan, ever since the days spent at the Court of France, as the child-betrothed of Charles VIII. In the Low Countries the fame and cult of Joan of France flourished exceedingly. Many ladies came to join the order, and further foundations were made at Bethune, Louvain and Alost.

Meanwhile in France also it continued to spread. The house at Rodez was opened in 1519. It was in this convent that Gabriel-Maria died, faithful in his last moments to the Order of the Virgin Mary.

Towards the end of his life he suffered great pain, but refused to give up any of his priestly work. All through the Lent of 1532 he continued to preach at each Mass, hear Confessions, and give counsel and direction. After Easter he set out to attend the Chapter of his Order, but was taken very ill on the way, and brought into the convent at Rodez. The sisters tended him with the greatest love and care, but he grew steadily weaker.

On the feast of St. Anne, July 26th, he said Mass for the last time, being unable to stand without support. After that he continued to hear Mass and receive Holy Communion. On the day of his death he managed to get to the church and say Matins, sitting in a chair. At dinner, after his usual custom, he put some questions regarding our blessed Lady; but excused himself from answering them, as his breathing was so distressed. Very soon, he said, *she* would give him the answers herself.

His last prayer was our Lady's *Magnificat*; it had always been his favourite. He never preached a sermon, Frances Guyard says, in Advent or Lent, without introducing into it one of the verses of this canticle. He died on August 27th, 1532, having survived his saintly penitent twenty-seven years.

In 1561, when Frances Guyard was busy on her chronicle, the Order of the Annonciade numbered ten convents, five in France, five in Flanders, Artois and Lorraine; but only a year later, still in the lifetime of Marguerite Blandine, it received a second terrible blow. The Wars of Religion broke out.

The Protestant Reformation had spread to England. In France, Calvin was terminating his disastrous career, and the evil passions of men had been fanned to a fury. Here, as elsewhere, the Blessed Virgin and everything connected with her were singled out for attack. When the Huguenot armies entered Bourges, the sisters were forced to scatter and hide. A troop of men made their way into the convent and wrecked the church. Some of them entered the vault and broke down the casket containing the saint's remains. They may have expected to find treasure. What they did find gave them a shock—a nun lying there, apparently quietly asleep.

The man who first laid hand on her recoiled in fear. It seemed to him that she breathed a gentle sigh! Others, more hardened, dragged the body out, stabbed it with their knives—it bled fresh blood, the bystanders declared. The crowning horror came when they carried it out into the courtyard, threw it upon a pile of wood, and set the whole alight.

Peace came again to France, and to the Order of the Blessed Virgin Mary. There were many more vocations, many more convents. By popular acclamation, Joan was proclaimed Saint. She was represented with the halo, her name was included in the litanies.

In 1604 a movement was set on foot to take up her cause in Rome, with a view to securing a formal and regular Beatification. The Archbishop of Bourges, who initiated the proceedings, was André Fremiot. He was the brother of Madame de Chantal—another Jeanne destined to be raised to the altars of the

Church—St. Jane Frances de Chantal. She was engaged at this time, in company with St. Francis de Sales, in founding the Order of the Visitation.

The Archbishop set to work to collect all the testimony and documents relating to the cause of Joan of France, known at this time, since another royal branch, the Bourbon, occupied the throne, as Joan of *Valois*. Petitions on her behalf came pouring in to the Holy See. The King of France, Louis XIII, the Spanish Infante, Governor of the Low Countries, the universities of Bourges and Louvain, all alike begged for her beatification. The documents of the process were collected and forwarded to the Holy See.

The Pope at this time was Urban VIII, famous for the work he accomplished in regularising the *cultus* of the saints. There had been too many saints canonised by popular clamour. The decree made by Urban VIII in 1625 was to the effect that, in future, the title of Saint should be conferred, not by acclamation, but by the Holy See only, and that after a lengthy and searching process. An exception was made in cases where the *cultus* had already been in existence for more than a hundred years, and had been *continuous*, *public*, and *tolerated by the Church*.

The case of Joan of France fell within this category. All that remained was to offer proof to that effect.

Unfortunately, the cause dragged on too long. While testimony was being laboriously collected of a hundred and thirty-three miracles performed by the intercession of Joan, differences, due to Gallicanism, arose between the Court of France and the Holy See. The matter of the Beatification had to be dropped.

In 1731, Louis XV again took up the cause with Clement XII.

"Most Holy Father," he wrote, "We have long been aware that the depositions and documents drawn up for the Beatification of the venerable servant of God, Joan of Valois, Queen of France, and Foundress of the Order of nuns of the Annonciade, have amply testified to the sanctity of her life and the miracles which it has pleased God to perform at her intercession: and some time ago we charged our Cousin, the Duke of St. Aignan, our Ambassador-Extraordinary to your Holiness, to solicit a speedy end to these proceedings. We were constrained thereto by the knowledge we have of the sentiments of piety inspired in all our subjects, inspired by their consideration of the virtues with which God adorned her, and her manner of exercising them, both on the throne and in the religious state. The daily augmentation of this popular sentiment on the part of our people, and particularly in the Order which she founded, gives us ever increasing concern to do all in our power to procure them the fulfilment of their desire: that your Beatitude having proclaimed her to be among the number of the Blessed, they may be free with confidence to invoke the aid of one whom they have always held in veneration. Most earnestly we supplicate your Holiness to defer this Beatification no longer."

On receipt of this letter, the Holy See requested that the necessary testimony should be collected anew. Accordingly a fresh process was prepared, setting out abundant proof that the *cultus* rendered to Joan had been public, constant, and approved by every Archbishop in Bourges since the day of her death. On June 18th, 1742, Pope Benedict XIV ratified the cult accorded from time immemorial, and under the special conditions laid down by Urban VIII, declared her *Blessed*.

Efforts then went on to bring about the final stage, her recognition as *Saint*. The process went forward. In 1775 the Canonisation was promised, Pope Pius VI going so far as to give permission, in France alone, for the celebration on February the fourth of the feast of *Saint* Joan of Valois. Then came the third blow, the French Revolution. During those turbulent years, not only were lost all the documents collected with such labour for the Cause of Canonisation, but every one of the convents of the Annonciade, without a single exception, perished.

Against these religious of the Blessed Virgin, many of them daughters of noble houses, the Terror raged with the greatest ferocity. They were forced to disperse and go into hiding, disguised in secular dress. Many of them displayed great heroism. Some of them suffered martyrdom.

Heroic indeed were the nuns of Villeneuve-sur-Lot. Here, in the days of the Terror, the sisters, their chaplain also, were living in hiding. It was after the decree which sought to compel every priest, under pain of expulsion from his benefice, to take the oath of loyalty to the Republic. Such an oath entailed schism from the Church.

The Franciscan friar who was chaplain to the nuns saw with sorrow that their fellow-townsmen were following their pastor into schism. It seemed to him that the time had come to put away concealment and stand witness to the truth. He communicated his design to some of the nuns, with the result that, the following Sunday, as the bells of St. Catherine's rang out for Mass, the people of Villeneuve-sur-Lot beheld a spectacle unusual in those days: a friar, in his habit and barefoot, walking along the street, and behind him, hands joined and eyes cast down, three nuns in the grey habit, the scarlet scapular, and the white cloak of the Order of the Blessed Virgin Mary. Unchallenged, they entered the church. The friar mounted the pulpit, and in his own name and that of the sisters, made a solemn declaration of Faith, affirming their loyalty to the Holy, Roman, Catholic and Apostolic Church. Having concluded, he made the Sign of the Cross, and the four quietly walked out of the church, and went and gave themselves up to the tribunal. Their subsequent fate is unknown.

It was very unfortunate that at this time, when the best hope of survival for the order lay in their convents outside France, the Emperor Joseph II saw fit to suppress, in the Low Countries, all religious houses except those engaged in teaching or nursing. This hit hard at the Annonciade, an order purely contemplative. Joan had expressed a wish that her daughters should not engage themselves in teaching, for she feared that it would prove a distraction from their proper vocation. Under the altered circumstances, however, the *Mère Ancelle* of Tirlemont felt justified in offering to set up a school. Her offer was accepted, and Tirlemont alone of the convents in the Low

Countries survived, until it too succumbed under French occupation during the Napoleonic Wars.

"I am sure that the gates of Hell will never prevail against the Order of the Virgin Mary," said Gabriel-Maria: "if you do not, of your own fault, ruin what Jesus and Mary have accomplished in you, there is no power in the world which can destroy it."

The gates of Hell seemed indeed to have prevailed, but only for a day. The Terror passed, and two convents, those of Villeneuve-sur-Lot and Boulogne, rose from the ruins. A few surviving nuns gathered together and re-established their communities.

The convent at Boulogne owed its resurrection to the fervour of two of its members. Bernadine de Celers, in religion Sister Mary of St. Cecilia, had to flee from France during the Terror, and take refuge, first in Antwerp, afterwards in Germany. One night, in the Rhineland, finding herself without shelter and penniless, she made a vow to the Sacred Heart that if she should be preserved she would, at whatever cost to herself, re-establish her convent at Boulogne. When she came back there several years later, she discovered one who had been in the novitiate with her. Sister Mary Godeleine had had an even narrower escape from death; for she was to have gone to the guillotine on the very day that Robespierre fell! The two of them managed to trace twelve of their old companions, and in 1818, with great jubilation, they re-opened their convent with a community of thirty religious.

At the earnest wish of their bishop, under whose jurisdiction they now came, they permitted some of their number, while preserving as far as possible the spirit of contemplation, to engage in teaching. When the anti-clerical law of 1901 expelled the teaching Orders from France, this community came under the order. The Convent of Boulogne went overseas, and established itself in England, at St. Margaret's Bay, near Dover.

The war of 1914–1918 brought about a great shortage of teachers in France. The ban against the teaching Orders was lifted, and the nuns in England were free to return to France. Some of them did so, and became established at Thiais, near Paris; but they left behind them a flourishing community, reinforced by vocations from among Englishwomen, at St. Margaret's Bay.

Two convents in France, Villeneuve-sur-Lot and Thiais, three in Belgium—for Tirlemont was re-established and now has two daughter-houses—one in England: these represent to-day the Order of the Blessed Virgin Mary. In these six convents is preserved the spirit of St. Joan of France, and the rule of life she gave them: a life of contemplation in which each religious strives, by the grace of God, to model herself upon Mary, cultivating the virtues Mary displayed on earth, so that they may give our Lord the service most pleasing to him. To think no evil, speak no evil, work no evil; to bear the sufferings of life in union with the sufferings of Christ and his Mother; to have no other treasure, seek no other joy but him who is ever waiting to console us in the Blessed Sacrament of the altar: this is the shining light of the Order of Peace, which radiates from those six centres, the convents of the Annonciade.

The Order of the Blessed Virgin Mary, the Order of Peace: what part are these destined to play in the days that are to come? A great one, surely; for to-day God is setting upon them the seal of his love and approval. After much tribulation, after many set-backs and disappointments, he deigns at last to grant the favour so long desired: the raising to the altars of the Church of her who founded these Orders, the holy woman who prayed, loved, and suffered long ago: St. Joan of France.